I am happy to recommend to you t  With Jesus to Israel. Just as Israel is ......... ...... ...... with milk and honey," this personal guide to Israel flows with information and inspiration. Its author has diligently labored to mix the elixir of the amazing with the necessity of biblical accuracy. The reader will be blessed and enriched by the historical and biblical background to each site visited. In addition, the "Points from the Pastor" feature provides extremely practical suggestions and helpful hints to get the most out of your travel experience.

As the title suggests, this handy guide—like the Bible itself—is all about Jesus. May God bless you as you walk in the footsteps of the Middle East's most famous son, Jesus of Nazareth!

VICTOR KNOWLES
Founder & President of Peace on Earth Ministries

Dudley Rutherford has spent more time in the Holy Lands than many of the Sabras who live there. His keen observation and insights bring a greater level of understanding than most travel information sources can offer. He gives the historical background to many of the major cities and sites, which lend themselves to a greater understanding of their place and time in the Holy Land and the world. His book allows the reader to see through his eyes the places where the important events of biblical history took place and how they affected the events we've read and heard about all of our lives. A major achievement, this book brings a wealth of knowledge to all who have found the joy in reading it.

LARRY MARCUS
President of Creative Travel Partners, Inc.

Dudley has provided much more than a personal tour guide for travelers to Israel. This is a perfect blending of education, inspiration, and discovery of the places, sights, and meaning in the Holy Land. He joins the many voices that have called out throughout history with the story of Jesus step by step. A necessary companion for the traveler in the land of the Bible and a valuable tool for those who can only know Israel from the heart of a pastor.

PASTOR KEVIN DIECKILMAN
Executive Director, One Heart For Israel

I found this to be an insightful writing that incorporates the history and biblical foundations of why a person of faith will want to visit the Holy Land. It offers the reader an excellent guide through a number of Israel's notable Christian sites with a perspective that only someone with the background of Pastor Dudley can offer. This text will greatly assist travel planners preparing programs for Christian visitors, and it will provide good introduction to a prospective traveler wishing to prepare for the life-changing experience of personally visiting the Holy Land.

S. "Scott" Feinerman
Professor of Tourism & Travel and
Program Director of Hospitality & Travel at
West Los Angeles College

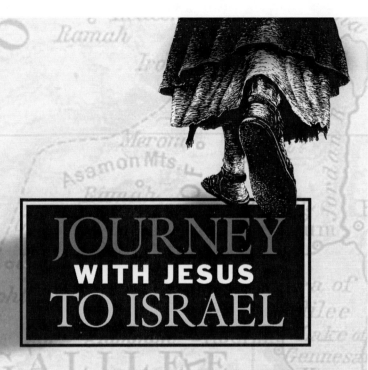

# JOURNEY
## WITH JESUS
# TO ISRAEL

*A HOLY LAND TRAVEL EXPERIENCE THAT WILL KNOCK YOUR SANDALS OFF!*

## DUDLEY RUTHERFORD

Published by Dudley Rutherford

Copyright 2012 Dudley Rutherford

Published in: United States of America

Content research, cover art, maps, book design and production: Steve Beaumont

# DEDICATION

This book is dedicated to the 1.5 million children who perished in the Holocaust and are honored at the Children's Memorial at the Yad Vashem Museum in Jerusalem. Their lives serve as a reminder of the importance of having the courage and conviction to support Israel's sovereign rights as a nation. May we always remember the children and the land of their forefathers.

DUDLEY RUTHERFORD

# ACKNOWLEDGEMENTS

Even though many years of hard work and diligent prayer went into the creation of this book, it was all worth it when I consider the thrilling experiences of my numerous travels to the Holy Land—which served as the catalyst for this great undertaking.

A book of this magnitude and detail could only be produced by a team of gifted and likeminded people, and I'm so thankful for the following individuals who shared my passion for the Holy Land and who helped make this project a reality:

First, I want to thank Steve Beaumont, from whom the idea of this book came about. Steve traveled with me to Israel several years ago and put together some material for his personal use. From there, we dreamed of writing an informative and inspiring book that would teach the traveler and non-traveler alike about Jesus and the land of Israel in which He walked. Responsible for garnering content and the meticulous task of designing the book, Steve never failed to demonstrate enthusiasm and commitment to the project every step of the way.

Next, I must express my appreciation for Angela Merrill, my writing assistant, who was integral to the research, writing, and editing of this book. Angela must moonlight as a professional juggler in her spare time—for there is no other explanation for her ability to keep so many of my projects in front of her at the same time, all while being a wonderful mother of two.

I must also thank my Shepherd of the Hills Church family (www.theshepherd.org) who has often traveled with me to the Holy Land. Our hearts have always grown closer to the Lord and to each other as we have trekked to Israel and back these many years. My preaching and their biblical understanding have been enhanced from having been in the ancient streets of Jerusalem and her surrounding cities and towns.

Beth Strahle volunteered her editing prowess in the critically important first copy edit and research phase. Thank you, Beth, for the gift of your time, kindness, dedication, and expertise. You are a wonderful blessing.

Many thanks to Connie Fogg, Freesia Parekh, Elizabeth Wozniak, and Denise Yasuda—the fantastic copy editors who put so much time and energy in ensuring we had our commas and semicolons in the right places and that our grammar, syntax, and spelling were up to par.

Finally, I want to thank the people of Israel—God's chosen people—who have endured and overcome so much and are a shining testament to the faithfulness of the Lord who always keeps His promises (Genesis 18:18-19). Thank you for always welcoming visitors into your beautiful, historic, and holy country.

*Dudley Rutherford*

*Pray for the peace of Jerusalem: "May those who love you be secure.
May there be peace within your walls and security within
your citadels." For the sake of my brothers and friends, I will say,
"Peace be with you." For the sake of the house of the Lord our God,
I will seek your prosperity.*

Psalm 122:6-9

# TABLE OF CONTENTS

# Foreword From Pastor Dudley

The phrase "a trip of a lifetime" is an understatement for anyone who tries to adequately explain his or her visit to Israel—the land the Bible describes as flowing with milk and honey (Leviticus 20:24). If you are fortunate enough to embark on this journey personally, you will discover quickly that there is a spiritual connection like no other when you see firsthand the sights and sounds of this region. It is much more than a vacation or holiday retreat. It's a much deeper experience in which God gives you the opportunity to walk where Jesus walked, to visit the locations of His many miracles and, of course, to visit the Garden Tomb where He was buried, seeing for yourself the etching above the empty grave that reads "He is risen."

Having traveled to Israel close to a dozen times, I have acquired an increased burden for everyone to have a chance to visit this incredible country as well. That's because I know that an odyssey to the Holy Land will change you forever—for there is no other place in the entire world that has such a potential to impact your life for all of eternity.

This book has three key components that make it an essential guide for your trip or for your studies. Throughout the many places that are highlighted in each chapter, you will glean:

1  *The historical background of every city* – pivotal moments such as the site's beginnings, any wars waged in the area, notable rulers, etc.

2  *The biblical background* of any site that is referenced in the Old Testament and/or New Testament, as well as its spiritual significance or application.

3  *Points from the Pastor*, which imparts to you words of wisdom you might not know otherwise when traveling to a particular site. This section also includes information and tips I've learned

from my many trips to the Holy Land and from the expertise
of different tour guides I've had the privilege to meet.

 Additionally, keep an eye out for this "Ask Your Guide"
symbol sprinkled throughout the book, which indicates
suggested sites or artifacts you'll want to ask your guide
to point out to you as you travel throughout Israel.

The unique elements listed above will enhance your travels and enable
you to gain the most from your experience. You'll hear so many details along the way that it's easy for all the facts to blend together, but
having this handbook at your fingertips will be a constant resource for
you—painting a clear picture of every location. It's your own personal
guide to the Holy Land! And whether you are literally on your way
to Israel or you simply desire to learn more about the place Jesus'
ministry originated, you will acquire not only godly wisdom from
this book, but also a love for God's people and the land He gave to
them. You will see history, drama, Scripture, biblical stories, and
adventure as God opens your eyes to spiritual truth that will knock
your sandals off!

## A Fresh Insight

You will never read the Scriptures the same way, because the Old and
New Testaments truly come alive after you've actually been to these
places. What were once black words on white paper now jump off the
page in living, high-definition color. You will now know what the Sea
of Galilee looks like, what Megiddo looks like, what Mount Carmel
and Nazareth and Bethlehem look like. You will have experienced
the Mount of Olives, to which David fled from Absalom and where
Jesus delivered the preeminent Olivet discourse. You will gaze upon
the Red Sea where the Israelites walked across safely on dry ground
by God's miraculous provision, and you will touch the cool waters of
the Jordan River in which Jesus was baptized. You will have a better
understanding of world history, but more important, you will have a
better understanding of how the very roots of the Christian faith are
intertwined with the Lord's promises to the Jewish people.

Every step of this journey will awaken your senses. You will learn
and experience more than you could ever imagine. And as you walk

throughout Israel, a place so rich in biblical history, it is amazing to know that there is always another world just below your feet:

*"Standing on the Cardo, an unearthed Roman main street in Jerusalem, one can see, in the banks of the excavation, soils from 6,000 years of history. For example, there is a sign in a nearby archaeological project that reads, 'You have descended three meters below the level of the present Jewish Quarter. You have gone back two thousand years in time.'"* [1]

But before we dive into our first travel day, I'd like to share some helpful hints to maximize your time in Israel. These are the best and most important lessons I've learned from my many visits to this marvelous country:

1  *Stand close to your guide* – Wandering away from your group to take photos on your own can be very tempting when you're surrounded by such beautiful and intriguing sights. But the closer you stick to your guide, the more you'll learn about each location. Whenever I'm in the Holy Land, I can always be found standing close to the travel guide because I don't want to miss out on the details he or she has to share. Remember, you will hear from some of the most knowledgeable tour guides in the entire world, so take advantage of this opportunity.

2  *There's water on the bus* – Many tourists find it helpful to know there is usually an ice chest at the front of the bus that is stocked with cold bottled water for about $1 – $2 each. Double check with your tour guide to be sure that your bus will in fact have water on board.

3  *Don't lag behind* – Trying to keep a large group of people together on a tour, while moving from point to point within a particular site, can be likened to "herding cats" because everyone is inclined to go in his or her own direction. When the tour guide moves to the next site, he or she has to wait until everyone catches up before beginning his or her discourse. I've been on trips where people lag 100 yards behind. So, out of consideration of others, please try to keep up. Remember that the group needs to move together to glean the most from your Holy Land experience.

4  *"Not everyone is holy in the Holy Land."* – This is a phrase that my

tour guide, who was an officer in the Israeli army, would say and the whole group would erupt in laughter. I've never forgotten that line and have used it many times myself. It's just a good reminder when you're traveling in Israel or anywhere in the world to use common sense, to be aware of your surroundings, and to be safe.

5   *Take good notes daily* – When you return home from Israel and peruse all the photos you took, you'll want to look over your notes and be reminded of what happened where. We've provided a section at the end of each chapter in this book for you to journal your thoughts. It will also help you to stick close to your guide to hear all the interesting facts.

6   *Look at your itinerary every day* – Most tour groups in Israel use different itineraries, so try to review your group's itinerary every evening to see where you will be going the next morning. Additionally, if you read the corresponding section of this book before you get to your destination each day, you will be better prepared for what God wants to show and teach you in the various sites and along the way.

7   *Pray every day* – Before you leave your hotel room each morning, pray that God will teach you something new—something that's life changing—during that particular day's tour. At the end of each travel day, thank God for giving you the resources and the privilege of seeing His Word come to life through the sights, smells, and sounds of these sacred places.

My prayer is that the above-mentioned tips and the rest of this book will prepare your heart, mind, and soul for the journey in which you will literally walk where Jesus walked. May you grow in your faith and be encouraged to live as Jesus lived—honoring God in all you do and say.

Enjoy—or, as they say in Israel, "Yehaneh!" ("yee-ha-NAY")

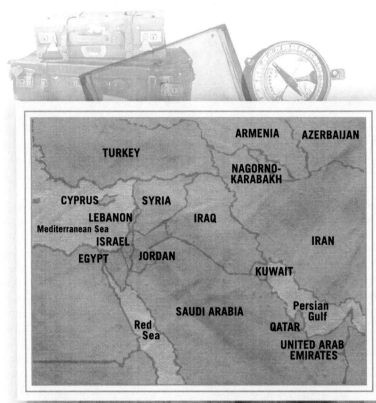

# Chapter 1: Travel To Israel

If you're sitting on an airplane heading to Tel Aviv, you have approximately 11-13 hours of flying time ahead of you. Once you arrive, there will be so much to absorb, from biblical and historical accounts to modern archeological discoveries, that it can easily become a blur. This book was created to help you get the most out of your trip to the Holy Land. At the end of each day, we've provided a few pages for you to journal your thoughts and to add your own notes on the historical background and biblical insights at each location.

This first chapter—although saddled with many details of the past—is important for you to read several times before you arrive. Doing so will enable you to have a richer, fuller experience. It's like looking at the image on the box of a 5,000-piece jigsaw puzzle, for this overview allows you to see the entire picture more accurately in order to fit together the individual pieces of information that will be thrown at you from city to city. Do your best to wade through Chapter One and get a good grasp of Israel's biblical and historical timeline. It might seem like more information than you need, but once you land in Israel, you'll be glad to know the particulars of these facts.

As we begin this journey, let's reflect for a few moments on God's unique relationship with Israel and then spend some time reviewing how the modern state of Israel came to be. It is important to understand that though Israel has an ancient, biblical history, dating back to about 2000 BC, the modern nation of Israel has only existed since 1948. And like any great story, it's best to start at the beginning...

## Standing on the Promises of God

*The LORD had said to Abram, "Leave your country, your people and your father's household and go to the land I will show you. I will make you into a great nation and I will bless you; I will make your name great, and you will be a blessing. I will bless those who bless you, and whoever curses you I will curse; and all peoples on earth will be blessed through you."* Genesis 12:1-3

The history of Israel begins with God's covenant with Abraham, Isaac, and Jacob, from whom the 12 tribes of Israel descended. God revealed to Abraham in Genesis 12:1-3 that a nation would arise from Abraham's descendants and that all people on earth would be blessed through him. While this is an outstanding promise, the Lord also made it clear that the Israelites were going to face some arduous challenges and steep obstacles along the way. Take a look at Genesis 15:13-14 to see the difficulties they would endure.

Despite this warning, Abraham and his offspring are assured in Genesis 12:1-3 that—no matter what happened—the Promised Land was a part of God's unwavering covenant (or promise) to them. By acknowledging this very special covenant, we begin to understand God's love for this country and its people. It gives Israel an identity as the people of Yahweh even to this day.

## Israel's Ancient History

Now, let's look at a quick overview of Israel's ancient history as well as a rough timeline, which will take us from Abraham, Isaac and Jacob to modern-day Israel. As we review the history, remember that the BC calendar runs backward, like a countdown clock.

Sometime between 2000 and 1500 BC, God changed Abram's name to Abraham and made a covenant with him:

*When Abram was ninety-nine years old the Lord appeared to him and said, "I am God Almighty; walk before me and be blameless. I will confirm my covenant between me and you and will greatly increase your numbers."*
Genesis 17:1-2

God's plan to increase Abraham's numbers started slowly. He and his wife Sarah had one son of the covenant, named Isaac (Genesis 17:19; 21:1-3). (Abraham's son, Ishmael, whom he had with Sarah's maidservant, Hagar, and the six sons of Keturah were not included.) Isaac had two sons with Rebekah—Jacob and Esau, which made them Abraham's grandsons (Genesis 25:25-27). Jacob, the younger brother, conned his older brother, Esau, out of his birthright and their dying father's blessing (Genesis 25:29-34). Years later, Jacob returned and made peace with Esau and at this point God confirmed Jacob's covenant relationship.

*God said to him, "Your name is Jacob, but you will no longer be called Jacob; your name will be Israel." So he named him Israel. And God said to him, "I am God Almighty; be fruitful and increase in number. A nation and a community of nations will come from you, and kings will come from your body. The land I gave to Abraham and Isaac I also give to you, and I will give this land to your descendants after you."* Genesis 35: 10-12

Jacob had 12 sons, who would later become the 12 tribes of Israel. (Now that's what I call "increasing in numbers!") Let's pick up the story with one of Jacob's sons, Joseph, who was the great-grandson of Abraham. Take a look at Genesis 37:3:

*Now Israel (Jacob) loved Joseph more than all his sons....*

Every parent reading this passage knows what kind of drama would be caused if you loved one of your children more than the others. In fact, many of you would probably say that to love one child more than another is impossible. This was not impossible for Jacob, and unfortunately, he didn't even try to hide his favoritism—giving a valuable, multi-colored robe to Joseph, which rightfully should have been given to the firstborn son. Jacob's obvious preferential treatment of Joseph caused his brothers to hate and become extremely envious of Joseph.

To make matters worse, Joseph began to have prophetic dreams that clearly showed he would rule over his brothers. In the first dream his sheaf of wheat stood upright while theirs bowed to his. In the second dream the sun (Jacob), the moon (Rachel) and eleven stars (his 10 brothers plus Benjamin who was yet to be born) were all bowing down to him.

The colorful coat was bad enough, but Joseph's dreams infuriated his brothers. Driven by jealousy, they tore off Joseph's cloak, sold him into slavery, soaked his cloak in animal blood and then told their father that his favorite son was dead. All this happened around 1897 BC. Next, Joseph had to endure hard work as a slave in Egypt in the house of Potiphar (an officer of Pharaoh), a false accusation from Potiphar's wife, and some undeserved time in a dungeon. Nevertheless, Joseph was soon exalted by Pharaoh to rule over the entire land, because Joseph so aptly interpreted the strange dreams the Egyptian king was having. Near the end of his story, listen to what Joseph had to say to his brothers:

| 2000 BC | 1800 BC | 1445 BC | 1200 BC | 1050 BC |
|---------|---------|---------|---------|---------|
| God changes Abram's name to Abraham. | Joseph sold into slavery by his brothers. | Moses leads Jews out of captivity. | Israel led by judges. | Saul becomes first king of Israel. |

*"You intended to harm me, but God intended it for good to accomplish what is now being done, the saving of many lives."* Genesis 50:20

Joseph realized that God had used him to save not only Israel but also Egypt from a seven-year famine, which you can read about in Genesis chapter 41. Amazingly, somewhere between 250 and 350 years later, the Egyptians enslaved Joseph's descendants, and around 1445 BC God sent Moses to lead the Jews out of this captivity. The Israelites spent the next 40 years wandering in the desert because of unbelief and disobedience. But finally, after an entire generation of people died off, around 1405 BC Joshua led Israel to take possession of the land God had promised them back in Genesis 12. We serve a God who always keeps His promises! Read Joshua chapters 3 through 6 to read this fascinating story of how Israel crossed the Jordan, took possession of the Promised Land, and defeated the city of Jericho with its fortified walls.

Over the next 400 years, Israel was ruled by a series of judges such as Deborah (Judges 4:4) and Samson (Judges 15:20), to name a few. This lasted until about 1010 BC when Israel began to pester God for a king. I can imagine that their pleas must have sounded something like this: "But God, all the other countries have one!" You've heard the phrase "Be careful what you wish for," right? Well, we see very soon the disastrous result of the Lord giving His people precisely what they asked for.

Around 1050 BC Saul became the first king of Israel, followed by David who reigned from about 1010 BC to 970 BC, then Solomon who reigned from about 970 BC to 931 BC. It was during Solomon's reign that the First Temple was built in Jerusalem. A description of the Temple can be found in 1 Kings chapters 5 and 6.

Next follows one of the most misunderstood subjects of Bible study:

| 1010 - 970 BC | 970 - 931 BC | 900 - 600 BC | 586 BC | 539 BC |
|---|---|---|---|---|
| David's kingdom. | Solomon's kingdom. | Israel splits into Israel and Judah. Time of the prophets. | Judah falls to the Babylonians. | Persia defeats Babylonians. Jews return to Israel. |

the political division of "Israel" and "Judah" that occurred after Solomon's death around 931 BC and during the reign of King Rehoboam. Before then, all 12 tribes of Israelites were a united kingdom through the reigns of both David and Solomon. But after Solomon's death, they split into two completely separate and independent kingdoms— the southern kingdom of "Judah," consisting of the tribes of Judah and Benjamin, with their capital at Jerusalem, and the northern kingdom of "Israel," consisting of the other 10 tribes: Reuben, Simeon, Dan, Naphtali, Gad, Asher, Issachar, Zebulun, Ephraim and Manasseh (Joseph was divided into Ephraim and Manasseh), with their capital in Samaria. The tribe of Levi had cities in both Israel and Judah.

Israel and Judah were never united again. Surprisingly, they even fought wars against each other from time to time.

From the 9th to the 6th century BC, Israel continued to move further and further away from God. During this 300-year span, God began sending prophets to warn them of the destruction that was to come if they did not repent from their sins, starting with Elijah, followed by Elisha, Obadiah, Joel, Amos, Hosea, Micah, Isaiah, and finally Jeremiah. However, the people did not heed these warnings, and God permitted both kingdoms eventually to be defeated by their enemies.

The northern kingdom of Israel fell first, conquered by the Assyrians. By 721 BC nearly all of the Israelites had been taken into exile (2 Kings 17:1-23). Most of them never returned; even today they are referred to as the "Lost Ten Tribes of Israel." About 150 years later, the southern kingdom of Judah fell to the Babylonians and the people of Judah were taken into captivity. The First Temple of God in Jerusalem was destroyed at this time, which was around 586 BC (2 Chronicles 36:17-20).

Nearly 50 years later, 539 BC, King Cyrus of Persia defeated the Babylonians and issued a decree stating that the people of Judah

| 520-515BC | 538-333 BC | 333-63 BC | 63BC - 333 AD | 70 AD |
|---|---|---|---|---|
| Israelites build Second Temple. | Israel under Persian control. | Israel under Greek control. Second Temple defiled. | Israel under Roman control. Jesus was born and lived to approx 31-33AD. | Second temple destroyed. |

could return to Israel. Not long after their return, which was around 520-515 BC, the Israelites built the Second Temple (Ezra 1:1-3; 6:14-18).

Despite the victory represented by this major achievement, Israel would be occupied by a long list of foreign rulers, and it would be approximately 2,500 years before the Israelites would officially take possession of their land again.

Here's a brief rundown of what happened during those sad, two-and-a-half millennia:

Persian control lasted for about 200 years, from 538-333 BC, followed by the Greeks who ruled for the next 270 years, from 333-63 BC. During this period, the Second Temple was defiled, leading to a revolt by a Jewish rebel army called the Maccabees. You see, after Antiochus IV Epiphanes, ruler of the Seleucid Empire, issued a decree forbidding Jewish religious practice, a Jewish priest named Mattathias refused to worship the Greek gods. Mattathias killed a Hellenistic Jew who stepped forward to offer a sacrifice to an idol in Mattathias' place— then he and his five sons fled to the wilderness. After Mattathias' death about a year later, his son Judah Maccabee led an army to victory over the Seleucid dynasty. [1]

Next came Roman rule, from 63 BC-333 AD. Jesus was born and lived during this era, and the Second Temple in Jerusalem was the one He walked amidst. When Jesus says in Matthew 24:2 "... *not one stone will be left upon another,*" it's the Second Temple He's talking about. During Roman rule, the Second Temple was destroyed (c. 70 AD) just as Christ predicted, and most of the Jewish population was sold into slavery throughout the vast Roman Empire. Parts of the Second Temple still remain, which you will visit and learn more about when you visit the Western Wall. Even after the destruction of the

| 636 AD | 636 - 1086 AD | 1086 - 1386 AD | 1386 - 1516 AD | 1516 - 1918 AD |
|---|---|---|---|---|
| ◯ | ◯ | ◯ | ◯ | ◯ |
| Byzantines pushed out by Arab invaders. | Muslim control of Israel. Dome of the Rock built on temple site. | Christian and Muslim Crusaders invade Israel. | Israel under Mamluk rule. | Ottoman Turks control Israel after defeating Mamluk rule. |

Second Temple in Jerusalem and the beginning of the exile, some Jewish life in the land of Israel continued.

From the 3rd to the 6th century AD, the Byzantines governed, but they were pushed out by Arab invaders around 636 AD. Muslims controlled Israel for the next 450 years, and during their reign the Dome of the Rock was built on the site of the destroyed Second Temple. Because this is such a holy site to the Jews, you can imagine how devastating this was to them. On the plus side, large Jewish communities were reestablished in Jerusalem and Tiberias by the 9th century.

For the next 300 years, waves of Crusaders—both Christian and Muslim—came to Israel in order to recapture the Holy Land. In the 12th century, many Jews were massacred by Christian Crusaders and many more were sent into exile. This ended when Egypt's Mamluk dynasty gained control of the area. During 200 years of Mamluk rule, the Jewish community rebounded as large numbers of rabbis and Jewish pilgrims immigrated to Jerusalem and Galilee. Prominent rabbis established communities in Safed, Jerusalem and elsewhere during the next 300 years. After ruling for two centuries, the Egyptian Mamluks were defeated by the Ottoman Turks who would control Israel from 1516 AD until after World War I (1918 AD).

Four thousand years of history is a lot to keep track of, so below we've sketched out a brief timeline. All dates are approximate:

| Timeline of Israel's History | |
|---|---|
| 2000 BC | Abraham gets a new name (Genesis 17:5). |
| 1897 BC | Joseph is sold into slavery (Genesis 37:28). |
| 1445 BC | Moses is sent to free the Jews (Exodus 3:7-10). |
| 1050- 1010 BC | Saul rules Israel (1 Samuel 13:1). |

| | | |
|---|---|---|
| ○ | 1010- 970 BC | David rules Israel (2 Samuel 5:4). |
| ○ | 970-931 BC | Solomon rules Israel. Under his rule the First Temple is built (1 Kings 6:1-14). |
| ○ | 900- 750 BC | Kingdom divides upon Solomon's death—the north becomes Israel, the south becomes Judah (1 Kings 11:34-42; 1 Kings 12:19-24). |
| ○ | 721 BC | Israel, the northern kingdom, falls to Assyria (2 Kings 17:6). |
| ○ | 586 BC | Judah, the southern kingdom, falls to Babylon. At this time the First Temple is destroyed (2 Kings 25:1-21). |
| ○ | 538-333 BC | Persian rule: Cyrus of Persia issues a decree allowing Jews to return to Israel from Babylonian captivity. During this period the Second Temple is built (c. 520-515 BC) (Ezra 6:14-18). |
| ○ | 333-63 BC | Greek rule: During their reign, the Second Temple is desecrated causing a revolt by the Maccabees. |
| ○ | 63 BC-333 AD | Roman rule: During their reign, the Second Temple is destroyed (70 AD) and Jews are sold into slavery throughout the vast Roman Empire. |
| ○ | 334-636 AD | Byzantine rule: The Byzantine Empire is Christian, so Jews are tolerated but lose many rights. |
| ○ | 636-1099 AD | Arab rule: During their reign the Dome of the Rock is built on the site of the destroyed Jewish Temple. |
| ○ | 1099-1291 AD | Crusades: Pope Urban II sends Crusaders to recapture the Holy Land. Jews experience great persecution at their hands. |
| ○ | 1291-1516 AD | Mamluk rule: Due to this Egyptian dynasty's tolerance, the Jewish population in the region increases. |
| ○ | 1516-1917 AD | Ottoman rule: During their reign, the walls of the Old City of Jerusalem are rebuilt. |
| ○ | 1917 AD-Present | Israel's modern history begins. |

Imagine that! For 2,500 years the Israelites were a people without a country. Fortunately, this isn't where the story ends. Through the prophets, God makes a profound promise to His people, that He will someday re-gather and reestablish the Jewish people as a nation:

*"See, I will bring them from the land of the north and gather them from the ends of the earth. Among them will be the blind and the lame, expectant mothers and women in labor; a great throng will return. They will come with weeping; they will pray as I bring them back. I will lead them beside streams of water on a level path where they will not stumble, because I am Israel's father, and Ephraim is my firstborn son. Hear the word of the LORD, O nations; proclaim it in distant coastlands: 'He who scattered Israel will gather them and will watch over his flock like a shepherd.'"* Jeremiah 31:8-10

*"...say to them, 'Thus says the Lord God: "Behold, I will take the people of Israel from the nations among which they have gone, and will gather them from all sides, and bring them to their own land; and I will make them one nation in the land, upon the mountains of Israel; and one king shall be king over them all; and they shall be no longer two nations, and no longer divided into two kingdoms. They shall not defile themselves any more with their idols and their detestable things, or with any of their transgressions; but I will save them from all the backslidings in which they have sinned, and will cleanse them; and they shall be My people, and I will be their God.'"*
Ezekiel 37:19-23

## ISRAEL'S MODERN HISTORY

By the early 19th century more than 10,000 Jews lived throughout what is today Israel. The late 19th century saw the growth of Jews returning to their homeland, largely due to Zionism—the international political movement that supports the reestablishment of a homeland for the Jewish people in Israel.[2] During World War I, the Ottoman Turks, who ruled over the eastern Mediterranean at the time, sided with the Central Powers (Ottoman Empire, Germany, Austro-Hungary, Russia, Bulgaria) and were defeated by the Allied Powers (Britain, France, the United States, Japan). So, after WWI the League of Nations put Britain in charge of the area. During this period of occupation, Britain signed the Balfour Declaration and later the British Mandate of Palestine, which stated that it was "in favor of the establishment in

Palestine of a national home for the Jewish people..."

There was a sharp rise in immigration in Israel as Jews fled persecution in Europe in the 1930s. In this 10-year period, 250,000 Jews returned to Israel. This rapid growth led to rioting by Arabs in Palestine. In an attempt to pacify the Arabs, Britain began to severely restrict Jewish immigration in 1939, but many Jews were desperate to escape Nazism and immigrated illegally.

After World War II, still facing persecution abroad, Jews continued to immigrate illegally, which led to an increasingly violent conflict with British authorities. In 1947, the British government withdrew from their commitment to the Mandate of Palestine, stating it was unable to arrive at a solution acceptable to both Arabs and Jews. There followed a period of continuous war until the United Nations approved the UN Partition Plan (United Nations General Assembly Resolution 181) on November 29, 1947, dividing the country into two states, one Arab and one Jewish. Jerusalem was to be designated an international city—a corpus separatum—administered by the UN to avoid conflict over its status. The Jewish community accepted the plan, but the Arab League and Arab Higher Committee rejected it.

On May 14, 1948, one day before the expiration of the British Mandate for Palestine, Israel declared its independence. Subsequently, five Arab countries—Egypt, Syria, Jordan, Lebanon and Iraq—attacked Israel, launching the 1948 Arab-Israeli War. After a year of fighting, a ceasefire was declared and temporary borders, known as the Green Line, were established. Jordan annexed East Jerusalem and what became known as the West Bank (meaning the west bank of the Dead Sea), and Egypt took control of the Gaza Strip. Israel was admitted as a member of the United Nations on May 11, 1949. During the war, 711,000 Arabs, or about 80 percent of the previous Arab population, fled the country. The fate of the Palestinian refugees today is a major point of contention in the Israeli-Palestinian conflict.

Since becoming an officially-recognized state in 1948, Israel has been on the defensive against continuous attacks from all sides: Lebanon is due north, Syria is northeast, Jordan is east, and Egypt is south. The nation of Israel is literally surrounded. In 1956 and again in 1967, Egypt tried to block Israeli shipping through the Suez Canal, which

led to brief wars and the Israeli occupation of Egyptian territory. Similar skirmishes have occurred with Syria, Lebanon and Jordan with similar results. Under the terms of the 1979 Israeli-Egyptian peace treaty, Israel withdrew from the Sinai Peninsula for the third time. It had already withdrawn from large parts of the desert area it captured in its War of Independence. In addition, Prime Minister Yitzhak Rabin and his successors offered to withdraw from virtually all of the Golan Heights, which border Syria in exchange for peace with Syria.

As part of the Oslo Accords, Israel withdrew from more than 40 percent of the West Bank and approximately 95 percent of the Gaza Strip. In fact, Israel has now withdrawn from approximately 95 to 100 percent, depending on whom you ask.

Negotiations continue regarding the remaining small percentage of the Gaza Strip of the disputed territories in Israel's possession. Israel's willingness to make territorial concessions in exchange for security proves its goal is peace, not expansion.

Here we are, 60-plus years from that May 1948 declaration of independence. Despite many attempts by every surrounding Arab neighbor to extinguish it, Israel continues as a representative democracy with a parliamentary system. The Prime Minister serves as the head of government and the Knesset serves as Israel's legislative body. The nation's economy is estimated as being the 17th largest in the world.[3] Israel also ranks high among Middle Eastern countries on the basis of human development, freedom of the press and economic competitiveness. Jerusalem is the country's capital, seat of government, and largest city, while Israel's main financial center is Tel Aviv.[4]

## SOME SIMPLE HEBREW PHRASES

Now that you've gained an understanding of the overall history of Israel and her people, it's important to have the attitude that we are here to be a blessing to this country while visiting. The people of Israel welcome our presence and appreciate us most when we try to understand their culture. Even making a small attempt at speaking the language goes a long way to making new friends. That being said, here are some simple Hebrew phrases that may be useful to you during your travels. Remember, as a general rule you stress the last or next-last syllable.

Hello: *Shalom ("shah-LOME")*

Good morning: *Boker tov ("boh-ker-TOHV")*

Goodbye: *Lehitra'ot ("le-HIT-rah-ott")*

Please: *Bevakasha ("be-va-ka-SHA")*

Thank you: *Toda ("to-DAH")*

Yes: *Ken ("kin")*

No: *Lo ("low")*

Excuse me/Sorry: *Slikha ("slee-CHAH")*

How much is it?: *Ma Hasha'a ("Mah ha-sha-AH")*

Help!: *Hatsilu! ("hat-SEE-lu")*

Where are the toilets?: *Eifo (Afo) ha sherutim?*
                        *("Ay-foh hah sheh-roo-teem")*

Do you speak English? (Male): *Ata medaber anglit?*
                                *("At-TAH med-a-bear ahng-LEET")*

Do you speak English? (Female): *At medaberet anglit?*
                                *(" Aht med-a-bear-et ahng-LEET")*

I don't understand (Male): *Ani lo mevin*
                            *("Ah-nee low mehveen")*

I don't understand (Female): *Ani lo mevina*
                              *("Ah-nee low mehveen-AH")*

How do you say...?: *Eikh Omrim...? ("Eye-ch om-reem")*

What does        mean?: *Ma ze        ?*
                        *("Mahzeh        ")*

Where's the bus?: *Eifo otobus? ("Eye-fo o-to-bus")*

Where's the boat?: *Eifo Oniya? ("Eye-fo oh-nee-ya")*

I'm Christian: *Ani notsri (t) ("Ah-nee-no-tsree (t)")*

Saturday: *Shabbat ("sha-BAT")*

Yesterday: *Etmol ("et-mol")*

Today: *Hayom ("ha-yom")*

Tomorrow: *Makhar: (ma-khar")*

# JOURNAL: TRAVEL TO ISRAEL

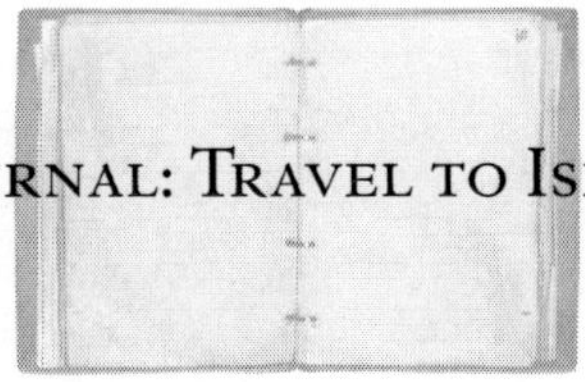

# JOURNAL: TRAVEL TO ISRAEL

_____

_____

_____

_____

_____

_____

_____

_____

_____

_____

_____

_____

_____

_____

_____

_____

_____

_____

_____

_____

_____

_____

_____

_____

_____

_____

_____

_____

_____

_____

_____

**Fact Finder**: *How many years did Abraham live?* Genesis 25:7

TEL AVIV
NETANYA
THE MEDITERRANEAN SEA
CAESAREA MARITIMA
MT. CARMEL

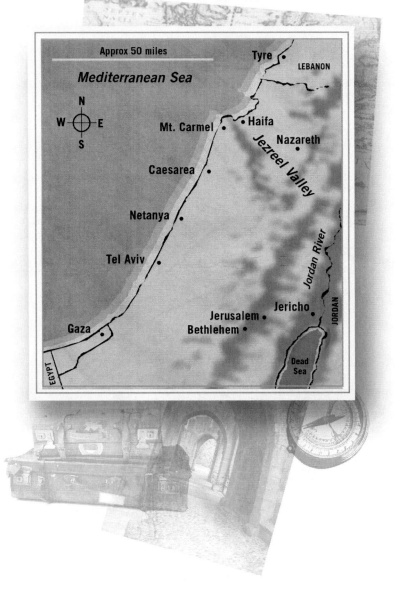

# Chapter 2: Mediterranean Coast

## Tel Aviv

We will be landing in Tel Aviv's Ben Gurion Airport, the country's only international airport, which is one of the most contemporary and well-secured in the world. Situated on the Israeli-Mediterranean coastline, Tel Aviv is home to approximately 3.3 million residents.[1] About 90 percent of Israel's entire population lives within a 90-minute drive of Tel Aviv's border.

Tel Aviv's Ben Gurion Airport                          *Photo: Dudley Rutherford*

Tel Aviv was founded in 1909 on the ancient port city of Jaffa. Today, it's a modern, "global city," meaning that it has been deemed as an important intersection in the global economic system.[2] Tel Aviv is the financial capital and business center of Israel, home to the Tel Aviv Stock Exchange, corporate offices, and research and development centers.[3]

Besides being a major economic hub, Tel Aviv is also known for its abundance of entertainment, museums, art galleries, restaurants, and beaches that attract about 1.7 million foreign tourists each year.[4] It has been called "The City that Never Sleeps" with its 24-hour culture, much like New York City.[5] Tel Aviv possesses tall and numerous buildings, hustle and bustle, energy, speed, style, culture, and a metropolitan feel.

We usually don't spend much time in Tel Aviv because the purpose of our journey is to see the ancient biblical sights of Israel. But if you have some free time, I would highly recommend that you try to visit The Nahum Goldmann Museum of the Jewish Diaspora located on the campus of Tel Aviv University. Its purpose is to help us understand the dispersion and re-gathering of the Jewish people and has been re-garded as one of the most innovative museums in the entire world.

Additionally, the tour of Old Jaffa is an excellent choice. Groups meet at the Clock Tower on Yefet Street every Wednesday at 9:30 a.m., and meander through Jaffa's captivating ancient port, archaeological sites, renovated alleys, quaint flea market, and picturesque artists' quarter. The view of Tel Aviv's coastline from the Crest Garden (Gan Hapisga) lookout point is one of the best parts of the tour. You will also embrace the historical landmarks from the days of the Egyptians, Phoenicians, the Old and New Testaments, the Crusaders, Napoleon and the Turks.[6]

Mediterranean coastline                    *Photo: Dudley Rutherford*

## Netanya

Israel is full of unique things to see and do, and since tour schedules are usually packed, it is difficult to find time to just relax. If you can make the time, there's no better place to take a break than the beautiful beaches of Netanya. Although there are no major tourist attractions here, its location makes it a convenient stop—just one hour from Jerusalem, 30 minutes north of Tel Aviv and 20 minutes south of Caesarea.

Let's take a minute to look at this town's history. Like many of Israel's cities, Netanya started as a moshava. Moshavas were rural, agricultural outposts not much different than early American colonies. On December 14, 1928, a team led by Moshe Shaked started digging for water, and in February of 1929 they found it. Later that month, the first five settlers had moved in and had begun planting citrus groves. By June of 1929, they were able to divide up the land and the first 10 houses were built.

Just three years later, the settlement had grown to 100 people. In 1933, the British architect, Holiday, proposed a plan for Netanya to become a tourist city, and in 1933 the first hotel in the city, Tel-Aviv Hotel, was completed. It came just in time because one year later Netanya was about to experience a serious population boom.

It began in 1934 with one boatload of 350 European Jews desperate to escape Nazi persecution in their homelands. It turns out that Netanya's beautiful beaches were perfect for something besides swimming; the 8.7-mile long coastline was used to smuggle Jews into Palestine. By now the British were strictly prohibiting immigration, but between 1934 and 1939, 17 more ships came with their cargo of future citizens.

Two of the new immigrants who came into Palestine carried what looked like broken bottle glass. What they really possessed were uncut diamonds and their own knowledge; these two men were experienced diamond cutters.

In 1939, despite strict British Mandate immigration laws, the mayor of Netanya, Ben Ami convinced the British high commission to allow a handful of Jewish diamond cutters from Antwerp and Amsterdam to enter Israel. It would change the course of this little rural village. By the end of WWII, 5,000 refugees had been trained to be diamond cutters. How amazing is that?! Once again we see the principle that Joseph talked about in action. Remember what he said in Genesis 50:20, *"You intended to harm me, but God intended it for good..."* Jews, facing persecution and death, were forced to flee from their homelands, but they carried their skill and its money-making potential to this fledgling country. Today, Israel exports around seven billion dollars worth of cut diamonds to the world. It is one of the main exports for this country, which has no natural resources.

Modern-day Netanya houses a large population of English-speaking immigrants from the United Kingdom, USA, and Canada. In 2007, the city had a total population of 176,500 and is expected to reach a population of 350,000 by 2020.

For tourists, Netanya features a number of museums and galleries. The Well House is a museum that tells the early history of Netanya; it is located on a farm that was established in 1928 in one of the earliest buildings in Netanya. Other Netanya museums include:

*Tribes of Israel Pearl Museum of Yemenite Jewish Heritage*
*Shlomo Dror Art Institute*
*Diamimon Diamond Museum*
*Cliff Gallery*
*Gosher Gallery*
*Abecassis Gallery*
*Fourth Gallery*

---

Oftentimes after landing in Tel Aviv, Israel's second largest city next to Jerusalem, travel tours elect to head straight to Jerusalem, which is about an hour drive from the Ben Gurion Airport.

Depending on the time of arriving flights, tour groups may check into a hotel in Netanya, which is only about a 15-minute drive up the coastline of the Mediterranean. Personally, I think it's best to save Jerusalem for the latter part of our trip, because as they say, "It's good to save the best for last!"

After such a long flight, Netanya is a great place to stretch our legs and catch our breath before heading north into Caesarea and the upper areas of Galilee. And since it's literally on the water's edge of the Mediterranean Sea, it makes for a lovely and appropriate introduction to this wonderful country.

Wherever you spend your first night in Israel, take a moment and thank the Lord for your safe arrival and ask Him to give you a good night's rest before you begin an exciting day of touring in the morning.

## The Mediterranean Sea

Our first clue to the importance of the Mediterranean is its name, which literally means "in the center of the earth." This body of water has always been an important route for merchants and travelers. Even in ancient times, it created opportunities for trade and cultural exchange among different people groups of the region—the Mesopotamian, Egyptian, Phoenician, Carthaginian, Greek, Levantine, Roman, and Moorish. The history of the Mediterranean region is central to understanding the origins and development of many of today's modern societies.

All of these societies were shaped by their close ties to this sea, which provided a way of life, business trade, cultural exchange, colonization, and sometimes war. Access to this common sea also led to many historical and cultural connections between the ancient and modern societies around the Mediterranean.

Because so many people groups—each with their own language—border this sea, it has many names. In Modern Hebrew, it has been called Hayam "the middle sea," a literal adaptation of the German equivalent

Mittelmeer. In Turkish, it is known as Akdeniz, "the white sea." In modern Arabic, it is known as al-BaÐr al-Abyad al-Mutawassit, the "Middle White Sea." And, lastly, in Islamic and older Arabic literature, it was referenced as Bahr al-Room, or "the Roman Sea."

The Mediterranean Sea is an "inland ocean," extending from Gibraltar to the west, to Israel to the east. It touches Europe, Africa and Asia, and was the crossroads of the earth in ancient times. It is about 2,300 miles long, from 100 to 600 miles wide and has a depth of 14,400 feet at its deepest point, off Cape Matapan. It connects with the Atlantic Ocean through the Strait of Gibraltar, the Black Sea by the Dardanelles, and the Red Sea by the Suez Canal.

## Mediterranean Sea in the Bible

The Israelites were generally not a seafaring people during the time of ancient biblical history. They were, however, familiar with the Mediterranean Sea, which formed the western border of the land of Israel. It is sometimes called the "hinder sea" in the Bible, because if you stand on its shore and face east toward Israel, it is behind you. In the Old Testament it is sometimes called the "western sea," (Deuteronomy 11:24; Joel 2:20) or the "Sea of the Philistines" (Exodus 23: 31), but most of the time it is simply referred to as the "Great Sea" (Numbers 34:6; Joshua 1:4; Ezekiel 47:10).

King Solomon had cedars of Lebanon floated in rafts down the Mediterranean coast to use in construction of the First Temple (1 Kings 5:8-9). The apostle Paul traveled extensively on the Mediterranean Sea during his missionary journeys.

Picture a pebble being dropped into a body of water; imagine the ripples spreading outward in an ever-widening circle. These ancient civilizations are that proverbial stone, but the Mediterranean is the body of water that carried their impact outward to the world and even to our time.[7]

## Caesarea Maritima

*At Caesarea there was a man named Cornelius, a centurion in what was known as the Italian Regiment. He and all his family were devout and God-fearing; he gave generously to those in need and prayed to God regularly.*
Acts 10:1-2

Caesarea Maritima has a long history. Somewhere in the 3rd or 4th century BC, it was established as a harbor by the Sidonian king Abdashtart. The city was named Strato's Tower. It was named in honor of three Sidonian kings. It changed hands many times over the next 200 years but by 63 BC it was part of the Roman Empire.

Mark Antony gave the city to Cleopatra, but when Octavian (later called Caesar Augustus) defeated Antony at Actium on September 2, 31 BC, he gave the city to Herod the Great. (This is the same Herod who had all the male babies under the age of two in Bethlehem killed after Jesus was born. See Matthew 2:16-18.) Herod named the city after Caesar but there were many other cities with the same name so it became known as Caesarea Maritima, or "Caesarea by the Sea."

Caesarea street, amphitheater and aqueduct          *Photos: Melissa Robles*

Somewhere around 25 BC Herod the Great began an extensive building program. He was determined to create a thoroughly Roman outpost here, since the city was ideally situated for trade. Like any modern Roman city it would've had markets, wide roads, temples, a drainage system for sanitation, aqueducts for fresh water and luxurious public buildings. Every five years the city would host major sports competitions, gladiator games and theatrical productions, so a Roman amphitheater was a must.

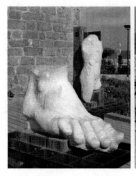

Caesarea Roman ruins and ancient harbor          *Photos: Melissa Robles*

There was one big problem with this new and improved city; its harbor had dangerous currents and tended to fill with silt. Never one to think small, Herod decided to build a 40-acre artificial harbor complete with a lighthouse (whose fire burned 24 hours a day), large breakwaters, six enormous bronze statues (used to mark dangerous sandbars), and anchorage for up to 300 ships. The harbor was built using materials that would allow the concrete to harden underwater. Some of the stones used to build the harbor's breakwater were 18 feet wide, 9 feet high and 50 feet long. Take a look at these other fascinating details:

> Its construction was an unprecedented challenge; never before had such a large artificial harbor been built. There was a total absence of islands or bays as natural protection; furthermore, work was hindered by bad weather. During preliminary underwater digs in 1978, archaeologists were stunned to discover concrete blocks near the breakwater offshore, an indication of the highly sophisticated use of hydraulic concrete, which hardens underwater. Though historians knew that the Romans had developed such techniques, before the discoveries at Caesarea, hydraulic concrete had never known to have been used on such a massive scale. The main ingredient in the concrete, volcanic ash, was probably imported from Mt. Vesuvius in Italy; it is likely that the wooden forms were, too. – Fodor's Israel [8]

The new harbor brought status and wealth to Herod's kingdom. He used the harbor to import materials for more building projects. Most importantly, it made Palestine easily accessible to Rome, only a 10-day voyage away. (Remember this fact and see "Points from the Pastor" at the end of this section.) An earthquake devastated this port in 130 AD.

By the time Herod was done, the city of Caesarea covered 165 acres. It boasted a 4,500-seat amphitheater, multiple temples, palaces, storerooms, residential areas, sewer system, public baths, paved streets, an elaborate villa that probably belonged to Herod himself, and a hippodrome that could seat 38,000 people. (The Staples Center in Los Angeles only seats 20,000!) Caesarea became not only the capital of the province, a role it played for the next 500 years, but also the headquarters for the Roman legions stationed in Judea. As you walk around, try to imagine what it was like while reading this account:

> It is almost impossible to imagine the splendor of the city and harbor, where the less noble building material was white limestone. Mosaic sidewalks, with long rows of columns, led from the city to the theater. Thousands of columns standing in parallel rows along the main streets formed majestic promenades throughout the city. More than 1,300 column fragments were found on the bottom of the harbor alone. They were made of marble imported from Italy and Egypt; columns of pink granite came from Aswan. Large slabs covered streets and sidewalks. Maritime trade was extensive: large warehouses facing the harbor contained... wine, olive oil, fruit syrups, and nails. The presence of Chinese porcelain attests to the geographical reach of Herod's commercial activities. – Jesus and His World[9]

Although the architecture of Caesarea made it quite impressive and beautiful, the social and political climate wasn't always peaceful. Imagine the following scene that took place between the palace and the stadium in 26 AD:

> Pilate, who was sent as a procurator into Judea by Tiberius, sent by night those images of Caesar that are called ensigns into Jerusalem. This excited a very great tumult among the Jews when it was day; for those that were near them were astonished at the sight of them, as indications that their laws were trodden under foot; for those laws do not permit any sort of image to be brought into the city. Nay, besides the indignation which the citizens had themselves at this procedure, a vast number of people came running out of the country. These came zealously to Pilate to Caesarea, and besought him to carry those ensigns out of Jerusalem, and to preserve them their ancient laws inviolable; but upon Pilate's denial of their request, they fell down prostrate upon the ground, and continued immovable in

that posture for five days and as many nights.

On the next day Pilate sat upon his tribunal, in the open market-place (the words may be translated, "great stadium," probably meaning our hippodrome) and called to him the multitude, as desirous to give them an answer; and then gave a signal to the soldiers, that they should all by agreement at once encompass the Jews with their weapons; so the band of soldiers stood round about the Jews in three ranks. The Jews were under the utmost consternation at that unexpected sight. Pilate also said to them that they should be cut in pieces, unless they would admit of Caesar's images, and gave intimation to the soldiers to draw their naked swords. Hereupon the Jews, as it were at one signal, fell down in vast numbers together, and exposed their necks bare, and cried out that they were sooner ready to be slain, than that their law should be transgressed. Hereupon Pilate was greatly surprised at their prodigious superstition, and gave order that the ensigns should be presently carried out of Jerusalem. " – Josephus [10]

As you can see, the Jewish and non-Jewish inhabitants of Caesarea often clashed. Under Roman rule, Jews were oppressed and their rights, laws, and traditions were ignored much of the time. Tension finally reached a climax during the desecration of the synagogue and the massacre of 20,000 Jews, which led to the first Jewish Revolt in 66-70 AD. Roman emperor Vespasian crushed this revolt and just one year later, his son Titus captured and destroyed Jerusalem and the Second Temple. Titus condemned 2,500 Jews to fight with wild beasts in the amphitheater in Caesarea in celebration of his brother Domitian's birthday. Caesarea also witnessed the execution of many of the Jewish captives of the second Jewish Revolt (AD 132-135) including Rabbi Akiva, one of the greatest religious leaders of Jewish history, who was executed along with all of his disciples. After the second Revolt was extinguished, Jews were exiled from Jerusalem and many chose to relocate to Caesarea.

Caesarea continued under Roman or Byzantine rule until 640 AD when Muslim Arabs captured the city and ruled until the 12th century. With their arrival, the harbor fell into disrepair and began to silt up. From the 12th to the 14th century, Caesarea bounced from Muslim to Christian Crusaders and back again. It was in the 13th century that the impressive Crusader fortress we see today was built by the French king, Louis IX. Despite its fearsome appearance, it offered ineffective resistance to the assault of the Mamluks who destroyed the city in 1265. (You will see these fortified walls and actually walk through the waterless moat as you enter Caesarea through the main Crusader gate.)

For hundreds of years after this final destruction, residents of other coastal towns used ships and boats to strip the city of its beautiful stonework and ruined structures. The aqueduct system, which had supplied Caesarea with water for more than 1,000 years and required constant maintenance and inspection in order to run smoothly, was neglected and soon became obstructed. The springs of water, no longer able to flow through them, turned the region north of Caesarea into a swamp, while the rest of the region was gradually covered by sand dunes. By the 16th century Caesarea was just a small, ruined village. Little that Herod had built remained.

The site remained abandoned until the Ottoman Turks resettled Muslim refugees from Bosnia there in 1878. The refugees fled the area in the 1948 conflict. The only surviving remnant of their village is the mosque, which can be seen near the sea.

These days, Caesarea is a thriving city with modern industry and 21st century conveniences. Israel's only golf course can be found here within a few miles of the Roman ruins.

## Caesarea in the Bible

After baptizing the Ethiopian eunuch, Philip was "transported" to Azotus (Ashkelon) and from there, continued to Caesarea, evangelizing as he traveled (Acts 8:40).

Under a death threat by Hellenistic Jews, new convert Paul was taken from Jerusalem to the port of Caesarea and shipped back to Tarsus (Acts 9: 28-29).

After Peter's vision about the clean and unclean, he traveled to Caesarea to share the Good News with Cornelius (Acts 10).

Paul's second and third missionary journeys sailed to and from the port of Caesarea (Acts 18:22; 21:8).

Herod Agrippa I died in Caesarea after "being eaten by worms" as God's judgment on him for receiving praise due only to the Lord (Acts 12:19, 21-23).

After his third journey, Paul stayed in the city with Philip and his four virgin daughters who were prophetesses. Paul then proceeded to Jerusalem with several disciples from Caesarea (Acts 21:9-16).

Paul was sent to stand trial before Felix and was put under house arrest in Caesarea for two years. While imprisoned he witnessed to Festus and King Agrippa and was eventually sent on to Rome (Acts 23-26).

**Fact Finder**: *From what Mediterranean seaport did Jonah depart?* Jonah 1:3

There are four significant ties to the New Testament in Caesarea— the impact of which is too great to measure:

1. In Jesus' day, Pontius Pilate lived in Caesarea and would have journeyed from here to Jerusalem for the Passover and the trial of Jesus. Up until 1962, we had no archaeological validation that Pilate had actually lived here until the famous Pontius Pilate stone was discovered. Now visitors can view a stone bearing his name, unearthed in a recent excavation:[11]

> Just inside the theater's main gate is proof that one of the Roman rulers who resided here was Pontius Pilate, prefect (governor) of Judea, when Jesus was crucified. It is the only archaeological evidence of the governor's presence in Palestine.... The fragmented Latin inscription on a mounted plaque reads: 'Pontius Pilate, the Prefect of Judea, has dedicated to the people of Caesarea a temple in honor of Tiberius to the Divine Augustus.'[12]

Make sure you ask your guide to show you the replica of this stone during your visit to Caesarea. The original is in the Israel Museum in Jerusalem. This archaeological find is important because, like so many other discoveries, this stone with Pilate's name inscribed validates the Scriptures and history of Christianity.

2. Acts 10:1-48 is one of the most critical passages in the entire Bible. It is the story in which Peter receives a vision to go to Caesarea and witness to a centurion named Cornelius, who was a devout man but had never heard the Gospel. This was, of course, God revealing that the Gospel was not just for the Jews, but also for the Gentiles. (If you are not Jewish, you would be classified as a Gentile.) The city of Caesarea should remind us of the importance that the Gospel of Jesus Christ is for people of all ethnic backgrounds. It was here Peter and the early Church leaders had to confront their prejudices, and from that moment forward, they began focusing on reaching all people—both Jews and Gentiles.

4,500-seat Roman amphitheater in Caesarea                    *Photo: Melissa Robles*

3. Part of your tour will include walking into the 4,500-seat Roman amphitheater, which is still in existence today and sits on the edge of the Mediterranean Sea. Upon entering the amphitheater, imagine one of the most dramatic events that ever occurred on the stage below.

To give some background, the emperor Tiberius wanted his friend Caligula to rule the region instead of Herod Agrippa, the grandson of Herod the Great. Because of this fact, Tiberius threw Herod Agrippa in prison. Sometime later, a fellow prisoner showed Agrippa a fierce-looking owl in the tree upon which Agrippa was leaning. Such an owl, called an "uhu" or "bubo," was rare to see in the daylight. The other prisoner told Agrippa that he would soon be delivered from imprisonment, promoted to the highest position of power, and envied by all who have pitied his misfortune. Continuing his prophetic discourse, the prisoner said that Agrippa would be happy until the day he died, that he would have children and they, too, would be happy. However, there was some bad news as well, according to the prisoner; the next time Agrippa saw the owl, he would die shortly thereafter.

Agrippa remained in prison during the short reign of Tiberius. Upon Tiberius' death and the accession of Caligula, Agrippa was not only set free, but (being favored by the emperors Caligula and Claudius) he acquired the provinces that had belonged to his uncle Philip and more territories were added to his kingdom so that he ruled over the entire region of Palestine, including Judea. When Agrippa had reigned three years over Judea, he came to Caesarea where he organized shows in honor of Caesar.

One day, Agrippa was informed about a certain festival in which vows were made for his safety, and there a great multitude of dignified persons gathered together. On the second day of this festival, Agrippa put on an extraordinary garment made entirely of silver, and came into the theater early in the morning. The sun illuminated the garment in such a surprising and resplendent manner that a look of horror spread over the faces of the multitude who cried out that he surely was a god. Upon this, the king did not rebuke the people or reject their impious flattery, but afterward, he looked up and saw an owl sitting on a rope over his head, and he immediately understood that this bird was the messenger of ill tiding and became deeply sorrowful.

Josephus, a Roman historian, records what happens next:

> A severe pain also arose in his belly, and began in a most violent manner. He therefore looked upon his friends, and said, "I, whom you call a god, am commanded presently to depart this life; while Providence thus reproves the lying words you just now spoke to me; and I, who was by you called immortal, am immediately to be hurried away by death. But I am bound to accept of what Providence allots, as it pleases God; for we have by no means lived ill, but in a splendid and happy manner." When he said this, his pain became violent. Accordingly he

was carried into the palace, and the rumor went abroad everywhere, that he would certainly die in a little time. And when he had been quite worn out by the pain for five days, he departed this life, being in the fifty-fourth year of his age, and in the seventh year of his reign. [13]

Acts 12:21-23 records this event as follows:

*On the appointed day Herod, wearing his royal robes, sat on his throne and delivered a public address to the people. They shouted. "This is the voice of a god, not of a man." Immediately, because Herod did not give praise to God, an angel of the Lord struck him down, and he was eaten by worms and died.*

You are standing in the very theater where this strange, historical and biblical event took place!

4. Wherever you are in Caesarea, you'll notice that you're literally on the water's edge. Look west, across the Mediterranean Sea, and imagine setting sail in New Testament time. You would be just a 10-hour boat ride away from Rome, the most powerful city in the world. Imagine being a resident of Caesarea during the time after Jesus' death, burial, resurrection and ascension to Heaven; the city is filled with both Jews and Gentiles, and the Gospel is being preached with great fervor and passion by some of the early disciples. It is from this magnificent port that the Gospel would one day travel across deep and capricious waters to Rome. Christianity advanced westward from where you're standing—the actual port of Caesarea Maritima—to Rome, then to all of Europe, and eventually to the New World.

If you could trace your spiritual roots far enough backward, they would originate from Caesarea Maritima, or "Caesarea by the Sea." Take a moment and be mindful of how God used this city-port—built by Rome for its own selfish purposes—to spread the Gospel to the known world. It is a very moving and powerful thought.[14]

# Mt. Carmel

*"Your head crowns you like Mount Carmel. Your hair is like royal tapestry; the king is held captive by its tresses."* Song of Solomon 7:5

Mt. Carmel's name comes from the Hebrew word, Karem El, which means "God's vineyard." Even today it's pretty easy to see why. In a mostly barren and arid land, this mountain appears positively lush and overgrown. Archaeologists have discovered ancient wine and olive oil presses here, which show the agricultural roots of this place. There would have been olive groves and vineyards dotting all across the mountainside. It was one of the most beautiful and fertile areas in Israel, which explains why it is used in Scripture as a symbol of beauty (Isaiah 33:9; 35:2).

In ancient and modern times, Mt. Carmel had another role. It acted as a border and a barricade. In Joshua 19:26, this four-to-five-mile wide range was used as the western boundary of the land allotted to Asher. But this 1,500-foot high limestone mountain range also helped to keep out unwanted intruders. Battles between Egyptians and Canaanites, British and Ottoman Turks occurred here and in the Jezreel Valley below.

Due to the caves, water and food sources, Elijah, Elisha, and Amos were all thought to have used Mt. Carmel as a refuge. In the 12th century, Carmelites founded a monastery on this mountain at the presumed site of Elijah's grotto. But without a doubt, Mt. Carmel is best known for one past event and one future event.

## Mt. Carmel in the Bible

It was right here on Mt. Carmel that Elijah challenged the prophets of Baal. In 1 Kings 18:24 we see him make his stand: *"Then you call on the name of your god, and I will call on the name of the Lord. The god who answers by fire—he is God!"* Never much of a diplomat, Elijah turns it up a notch in verse 27 taunting the prophets of Baal about their false god: *"Shout louder! Perhaps he's deep in thought, or busy, or traveling."*

You remember the rest of the story; their god (with a little "g") is a no-show, but Elijah's God (with a big "G") sends fire so fierce it licks up the sacrifice, the gallons of water, the stones and the soil. The people finally believe and follow Elijah's orders to kill all 450 of Baal's prophets. Elijah then climbs to the top of Mt. Carmel and prays for the Lord to send rain and end the drought. As you stand on this high place, try to picture the last verse in 1 Kings 18 with the rain pouring down, *"The power of the Lord came upon Elijah and, tucking his cloak into his belt, he ran ahead of Ahab all the way to Jezreel."*

On the northern slope of Mt. Carmel is Haifa, Israel's third largest city, but it is the southern slope that overlooks the Jezreel Valley. From this mountaintop you can see a battlefield more famous than Gettysburg and this battle hasn't even been fought yet! Below is the Valley of Armageddon.

Statue of Elijah and view over Jezreel Valley            *Photos: Dudley Rutherford*

Just like in Elijah's time, many false gods have staked their claim of the high places like Mt. Carmel. The Baha'i (a religion founded in Persia in the 19th century) and Druze (an offshoot of Islam) have temples here, and the largest mosque in Israel, Mahmood Mosque, is also located on Mt. Carmel. It is sobering to stand on this mountain and know that the God who destroyed the false gods in Elijah's time will someday return and destroy every false god once and for all. [15]

Elijah lived 900 years before Christ. His role was to bring the Word of God to Israel. He was associated with many miracles and the power of God, and he spent his entire life serving Yahweh, the one and only Almighty God. When he left the earth, he didn't die like many of the other prophets who were martyred. Instead, we learn that Elijah was walking down a road when suddenly a chariot of fire descended from the sky and took Elijah up to heaven in a whirlwind...and he was seen no more (2 Kings 2:1-11).

Because of this story, an expectation grew that Elijah would return one day to usher in the final stages of the world. In fact during Passover, some Jews would prepare a cup and leave an empty chair for Elijah in case he returned! This helps us to understand why people thought Jesus Christ was Elijah, as seen in Luke 9:18-20.

When you walk into the memorial area of Mount Carmel, you will see a statue of Elijah with his sword in the air and his foot upon one of the 450 prophets of Baal, which symbolizes the cleansing of wickedness from the land. When you gaze at this statue, please remember that even though it honors Elijah for slaughtering the 450 false prophets, the reality is that God is the one, true God and He alone was responsible for this great victory.

Additionally, perhaps the most important part of this story is that after Baal's prophets were defeated, the Lord God Almighty brought a "heavy rain" to the land after a terrible, three and a half-year drought and famine (1 Kings 18:45). This is a picture of God sending blessing, life, renewal, and restoration once men turn from their false idols and honor Him with their lives. It is an encouragement that one day, there will be a great and final battle, and the Lord will rid the world of every evil once and for all.

In the following chapter, we will discuss the biblical importance and relevance of the Battle of Armageddon (Revelation 16:16). For now as you stand on top of Mount Carmel, just take in this magnificent view and imagine the future battle that will be fought on the plain below. Certainly in that day, the mountain upon which you are standing will be a strategic vantage point for this great and impending conflict.

# CAESAREA / MT. CARMEL

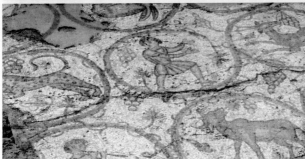

*Top left:* Wall at Caesarea's city entrance features arrow loops which allowed archers to fire at enemies below while mostly protected.

*Top right:* Many Roman statues still stand in Caesarea.

*Above:* Caesarea architecture details.

*Left above:* Mosiac bathhouse floor from Caesarea's Byzantine period – fourth to seventh centuries, AD.

*Left below:* Stone relief at Mt. Carmel depicts prophets of Baal praying to their god to send fire to ignite the altar.

*Photos: Steve Beaumont*

# JOURNAL: MEDITERRANEAN COAST

_____

_____

_____

_____

_____

_____

_____

_____

_____

_____

_____

_____

_____

_____

_____

_____

_____

_____

_____

_____

_____

_____

_____

_____

_____

**Fact Finder**: _What sort of spirits will be responsible for the gathering of armies at Armageddon?_ Revelation 16:14,16

# JOURNAL: MEDITERRANEAN COAST

JEZREEL VALLEY
MEGIDDO
ARMAGEDDON
MOUNT TABOR
CANA
NAZARETH
SEPPHORIS

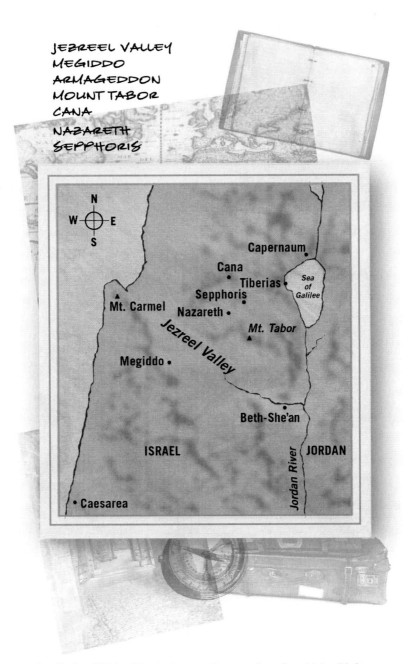

**Fact Finder**: *Which of the twelve apostles were from Cana?* John 21:2

# CHAPTER 3: JEZREEL VALLEY / LOWER GALILEE

## JEZREEL VALLEY

*Some time later there was an incident involving a vineyard belonging to Naboth the Jezreelite. The vineyard was in Jezreel, close to the palace of Ahab king of Samaria. Ahab said to Naboth, "Let me have your vineyard to use for a vegetable garden, since it is close to my palace. In exchange I will give you a better vineyard or, if you prefer, I will pay you whatever it is worth." But Naboth replied, "The LORD forbid that I should give you the inheritance of my fathers."* 1 Kings 21:1-3

Jezreel means "God sows." Thus, it should be no surprise that this valley is home to some of the most fertile farmland in Israel. Laurence Oliphant—British author, international traveler, and diplomat— eloquently described the valley in 1887 as "a huge green lake of waving wheat with its village-crowned mounds rising from it like islands." Rich in natural springs, this "breadbasket" supplies local needs and produces enough for export. This is Israel's heartland. It's no wonder that Ahab and Jezebel wanted Naboth's land.

Aside from its agricultural significance, the Jezreel Valley was an important thoroughfare even in ancient times as it presented an easy route from the ocean in the west to the mountains east of the Jordan River and to Egypt. In Scripture, this route is called the Way of the Sea (Isaiah 9:1). The Romans called it Via Maris, and in their time this route went from Egypt to Mesopotamia. Even today, the valley is a major artery for transportation to and from the port of Haifa.

In ancient times, this valley was also known as the Plain of Esdraelon. The central part is usually referred to as the Jezreel Valley and the southwest portion is known as the Valley of Megiddo (Armageddon).

## Jezreel Valley in the Bible

This valley has seen many battles. Here, Joshua defeated the Canaanites and allotted the land to Issachar. Here, the Midianites, Amalakites, and other eastern people were allowed to harass and oppress God's people for seven long years. Here, under a tree in the city of Ophrah, Gideon heard the angel of the Lord say, "The Lord is with you, mighty warrior" (Judges 6:11-12). Here at the spring of Harod, Gideon's warriors took their pass-or-fail drinking test, which reduced their number from 10,000 to 300 (Judges 7). But God gave the 300 a decisive advantage, for it was in this valley that those 300 men, armed with trumpets, empty jars, and torches, saw the Almighty One, the One true God, win the impossible victory for them. Also here in the Jezreel Valley, Saul and his army camped in preparation for their battle with the Philistines who had stationed themselves across the Harod Valley near Shunem (1 Samuel 28:4). And on Mount Gilboa, Saul and his three sons died (1 Samuel 28-31). Many battles have been fought on this plain, but it is still best known for the battle that is yet to come...the Battle of Armageddon.

## Megiddo

*Kings came, they fought; the kings of Canaan fought at Taanach by the waters of Megiddo, but they carried off no silver, no plunder.* Judges 5:19

Tel Megiddo means the "hill or mound of Megiddo." This hill was formed over a period of about 5,000 years. From around 6000 BC until 500 BC, Megiddo was destroyed and rebuilt over and over again. In fact, archaeologists believe that there have been 20 cities built on this site, each one piled right on top of the rubble left by the others. With each rebuilding, the city got a little higher.

Megiddo has always been a strategic place. It was one of three cities that provided guarded access to the Plain of Megiddo. Several major trade routes passed through Megiddo including the main route between Egypt and Mesopotamia. Whoever controlled Megiddo also controlled the traffic and trade. This brought great wealth and military power, but it also brought war—and lots of it. This broad plain has seen more than 100 battles, from Egyptians to Assyrians to Israelites to Napoleon. Four of the more famous battles are:

• The Battle of Megiddo in the 15th century BC was fought between the armies of the Egyptian pharaoh Thutmose III and a large Canaanite coalition led by the rulers of Megiddo and Kadesh. This is the first documented battle in recorded history. Think of all the wars that have ever been waged—the Battle of Megiddo was the earliest ever written about.

Megiddo ruins                                                    *Photos: Melissa Robles*

• Megiddo was destroyed in the military campaign of Pharaoh Shishak in 926 BC, and rebuilt during the reign of Ahab, king of Israel (c. 874-852 BC) who made it a royal "chariot city." Archeologists estimate that the stables could accommodate 450 horses and dozens of battle chariots. Solomon's gate into the city hung from fortress walls that were 11-feet thick with room for barracks and storage within.

• The Battle of Megiddo in 609 BC was fought between Egypt and the Kingdom of Judah, in which King Josiah fell (2 Kings 23:29-30).

•The Battle of Megiddo in 1918 was fought during World War I between Allied troops, led by General Edmund Allenby, and the defending Ottoman army.

On top of Megiddo, you will see a most impressive engineering feat, which was designed to protect the city's water source during a siege. Started by Solomon as a reservoir, Ahab made it more complex by having a subterranean tunnel cut, 80 feet deep and then 230 feet long, connecting the city to springs outside the city wall. The tunnel was cut from both ends simultaneously, and the engineering was so precise that when they met in the middle, they were only off by one foot. Finally, a thick wall covered by earth was built to hide the original entrance to the cave from which the spring came.[1]

You will be given the opportunity to walk down the stairs that lead to the tunnel, and it's good to note beforehand that there are many steps. Thankfully, most are descending, but make sure you're in good shape for the short trek. Don't ask me how it works, but after you exit the tunnel, the tour bus will actually be there to pick you up!

## MEGIDDO IN THE BIBLE

The city was originally Canaanite; in fact, the remains of a Canaanite worship center and its 5,000-year-old altar are still visible in the eastern part of the city. The Egyptian pharaoh Thutmose III took Megiddo from the Canaanites in 1470 BC and said, "The capturing of Megiddo is the capturing of a thousand cities." This conquest further established Egyptian presence and control of the land before the conquest under Joshua.

After the conquest and settling of the land, Megiddo became one of the major cities in the area that the tribe of Manasseh was unable to completely conquer. Eventually, God used Deborah from the hill country of Samaria and Barak from Kedesh to overcome the Canaanites of the region (Judges 4:13-15; 5:19-25).

Solomon fortified Megiddo, making it his stronghold to ensure his control of the territory (1 Kings 9:15-16). After Solomon's death, however, Shishak of Egypt destroyed Megiddo and erected a stone pillar on the site to mark his victory (1 Kings 14:25-28).[2] Later, in 874-853 BC, Ahab rebuilt the city in grand style. It was at Megiddo that Pharaoh Neco killed King Josiah in battle (2 Kings 23:29-30).

Megiddo served as the seat of the royal governor during the reign of

Jeroboam II, king of Israel (2 Kings 14:23). In the early 1900s a seal was found bearing the inscription "to Shema, servant of Jeroboam." During the rebellion of Jehu, King Ahaziah of Judah fled to Megiddo and died there of his wounds (2 Kings 9:27).

Megiddo was finally conquered and destroyed in 732 BC during the campaign of Tiglath Pilesser III, king of Assyria, against the Kingdom of Israel (2 Kings 15:29). This is Megiddo's past, but Armageddon is Megiddo's future.

## ARMAGEDDON

The word "Armageddon" is a derivative of the Hebrew word Megiddo, and many people believe that the final battle on earth will happen right here. It will be a culmination of the tension and struggle we have experienced since sin was ushered into the world—marked by intense, spiritual warfare like we have never seen before. Just look at how John describes the forces that oppose God as they prepare for this terrible time to come: *They are spirits of demons performing miraculous signs, and they go out to the kings of the whole world, to gather them for the battle on the great day of God Almighty...Then they gathered the kings together to the place that in Hebrew is called Armageddon.* Revelation 16:14,16.

However, other Scriptures suggest that this plain is not the site of the final conflict, but is instead a staging ground where the enemies of God will gather before they attack. For instance, Zechariah predicts that just before the Messiah's return, Gentile nations will come against Jerusalem to destroy it (Zechariah 12:1-9). Joel also predicts this attack on Jerusalem referring to "multitudes, multitudes in the valley of decision" (Joel 3:1-17). The climax of this attack will be Christ's return, when He will deliver the repentant remnant of Israel (Revelation 14). [3]

---

There have been many prophesies and interpretations about the events that will unfold during the Battle of Armageddon, as described in the book of Revelation. However, because Revelation was written in Apocrypha (or "coded") language, no one knows for certain the details of that day except for Almighty God.

POINTS FROM THE PASTOR

When engulfed in curiosity or simply desiring to discover truth, it's always best to read the Scriptures and to ask God to give you an understanding of His Word.

Please take a look at these important passages: Revelation 9:13-16; 14:20; 16:13-19; 19:11-21; 20:8-15. As you read through these passages there are several intriguing details:

First, Revelation 9:16 tells us that this final confrontation between good and evil, light and dark, God and those who oppose Him, will involve an army of 200 million soldiers. Some scholars argue that an army of that size today could only come from China. Second, Revelation 14:20 reveals that the blood will flow as high as a horse's bridle, for a distance of 200 miles. One reason not to take these details literally is that the Valley of Armageddon is only 14 miles wide and 20 miles long.

Opinions are varied and numerous, but one must note that the Scriptures have one thing in common; there is coming a day of ultimate judgment when Jesus Christ returns. So, instead of becoming consumed with trying to discover and decode the details of the battle, it is better to ask yourself if you are ready for Jesus' return. According to Acts 1:7-8, our Lord commands us not to be concerned about the dates and details of His return, but to be ready...and to share the Gospel with as many people as possible before He returns. Therefore, our concern should not be about the battle in this valley at the base of Megiddo, but our minds should be focused on the battle in our heart and in the hearts of others, and whether or not we're prepared spiritually for the coming Day of Judgment.

*Now, brothers, about times and dates we do not need to write to you, for you know very well that the day of the Lord will come like a thief in the night. While people are saying, "Peace and safety," destruction will come on them suddenly, as labor pains on a pregnant woman, and they will not escape.*

*But you, brothers, are not in darkness so that this day should surprise you like a thief. You are all sons of the light and sons of the day. We do not belong to the night or to the darkness. So then, let us not be like others, who are asleep, but let us be alert and self-controlled. For those who sleep, sleep at night, and those who get drunk, get drunk at night. But since we belong to the day, let us be self-controlled, putting on faith and love as a breastplate, and the hope of salvation as a helmet. For God did not appoint us to suffer wrath but to receive salvation through our Lord Jesus Christ.* 1 Thessalonians 5:1-9

*The Lord is not slow in keeping his promise, as some understand slowness. He is patient with you, not wanting anyone to perish, but everyone to come to repentance.*

*But the day of the Lord will come like a thief. The heavens will disappear with a roar; the elements will be destroyed by fire, and the earth and everything in it will be laid bare.*

*Since everything will be destroyed in this way, what kind of people ought you to be? You ought to live holy and godly lives as you look forward to the day of God and speed its coming. That day will bring about the destruction of the heavens by fire, and the elements will melt in the heat. But in keeping with his promise we are looking forward to a new heaven and a new earth, the home of righteousness.*

*So then, dear friends, since you are looking forward to this, make every effort to be found spotless, blameless and at peace with him.* 2 Peter 3:9-14

---

**Fact Finder***: What was the first public miraculous sign performed by Jesus Christ?* John 2:1-11

===

## MOUNT TABOR

*Then he asked Zebah and Zalmunna, "What kind of men did you kill at Tabor?" "Men like you," they answered, "each one with the bearing of a prince."* Judges 8:18

Located in Lower Galilee and just 11 miles west of the Sea of Galilee, Mount Tabor is 1,843 feet above sea level and actually visible from Megiddo. Have your tour guide point this out to you.

During the period of the Second Temple in Jerusalem, this mountain was used as part of a relay system that lit beacons to signal the start of the new month and holidays for those outside the city. At this height, you can see why.

Mt. Tabor

*Photo: Todd Bolen*

In 66 AD, during the first Jewish Revolt, the Jewish army retreated to Mt. Tabor but was later conquered by Vespasian's men. During the years of the Crusades, the site changed hands between the Muslims and Christians many times.

Origen, in the 3rd century AD, was the first to identify Mt. Tabor as the Mount of Transfiguration depicted in Matthew 17, Mark 9, and Luke 9. The Bible does not name this precise location; it only describes it as a "high mountain." Some said Mt. Tabor was the site of the transfiguration while others argued it was Mt. Hermon. In 348 AD the bishop of Jerusalem declared Mt. Tabor the winner.

Today there are two Christian monasteries on Mt. Tabor; one is Greek Orthodox and the other is Roman Catholic.

## Mount Tabor in the Bible

This mountain is first mentioned in Joshua 19:22 as part of the boundary of Issachar's land and the border of three tribes: Zebulun, Issachar and Naphtali. Mt. Tabor is next mentioned in the book of Judges where Deborah the prophetess summoned Barak of the tribe of Naphtali and gives him God's command:

*"Go, take with you ten thousand men of Naphtali and Zebulun and lead them up to Mount Tabor."* Judges 4:6

As promised by God, through Deborah the Canaanites were destroyed. Gideon names Mt. Tabor as the site of his brothers' death at the hands of the Midianite kings, Zebah and Zalmunna (Judges 8:18). And, if Origen and the bishop of Jerusalem figured correctly, Mt. Tabor may actually be the "high mountain" where Christ was transfigured. As believers we talk about having "mountaintop" experiences in our spiritual journey with the Lord, but this was literally a mountaintop experience. Notice Peter's reaction in the passage; he wanted to pitch some tents and stay there forever, but that was not God's plan for Peter and it probably will not be His plan for us.

## The Transfiguration

*After six days Jesus took with him Peter, James and John the brother of James, and led them up a high mountain by themselves. There he was transfigured before them. His face shone like the sun, and his clothes became as white as the light. Just then there appeared before them Moses and Elijah, talking with Jesus.*

*Peter said to Jesus, "Lord, it is good for us to be here. If you wish, I will put up three shelters—one for you, one for Moses and one for Elijah." While he was still speaking, a bright cloud enveloped them, and a voice from the cloud said, "This is my Son, whom I love; with him I am well pleased. Listen to him!"*

*When the disciples heard this, they fell facedown to the ground, terrified. But Jesus came and touched them. "Get up," he said. "Don't be afraid." When they looked up, they saw no one except Jesus.*

*As they were coming down the mountain, Jesus instructed them, "Don't tell anyone what you have seen, until the Son of Man has been raised from the dead."* Matthew 17:1-9 (Also found in Mark 9:2-9 and Luke 9:28-36.)[4]

# CANA

Although modern scholars are not so sure, the Vatican in the 17th century officially recognized Kafr Kanna as ancient Cana, and in 1879 the Franciscans built a church on this traditional site of Jesus' first miracle, which took place at a wedding (see John 2:1-11 next page). The church, with its twin towers, was modeled after the cathedral in Salzburg, Austria. Not to be outdone, the Greek Orthodox built the Church of Saint George right next door, which houses two of the stone jars they believe Jesus used when He turned water into wine.

In 1997, excavations uncovered a 14th century church beneath the Franciscan church. As the dig continued, more was uncovered including a funerary chapel from the 5th or 6th century and a mosaic floor from the 3rd century which reads "Remember Joseph, son of Tanhum, son of Butah with his sons because they made this tabula: may they be blessed. Amen." The mosaic floor suggests that there may have been a Jewish synagogue here once.

We may not have ancient Cana's GPS coordinates, but the most accepted tradition, which says this is the site of Jesus' first miracle, has led to a new tradition. Today, many come here to propose, to get married, or to renew their wedding vows.

## Cana in the Bible

Just as it is nowadays, the ancient world had major, influential cities where people from miles around came to do business: Rome, Damascus, Jerusalem, and Athens. Cana was not one of them; however, as stated before, its greatest claim to fame is that shortly after being baptized in the Jordan River, Jesus performed His very first miracle here:

*On the third day a wedding took place at Cana in Galilee. Jesus' mother was there, and Jesus and his disciples had also been invited to the wedding. When the wine was gone, Jesus' mother said to him, "They have no more wine."*

*"Dear woman, why do you involve me?" Jesus replied, "My time has not yet come."*

*His mother said to the servants, "Do whatever he tells you."*

*Nearby stood six stone water jars, the kind used by the Jews for ceremonial washing, each holding from twenty to thirty gallons.*

*Jesus said to the servants, "Fill the jars with water." And they filled them to the brim.*

*Then he told them, "Now draw some out and take it to the master of the banquet."*

*They did so, and the master of the banquet tasted the water that had been turned into wine. He did not realize where it had come from, though the servants who had drawn the water knew. Then he called the bridegroom aside and said, "Everyone brings out the choice wine first and then the cheaper wine after the guests have had too much to drink; but you have saved the best till now."*

*This, the first of his miraculous signs, Jesus performed in Cana of Galilee. He thus revealed his glory, and his disciples put their faith in him."* John 2:1-11

Cana's second, important biblical mention is as follows:

*Once more he visited Cana in Galilee, where he had turned the water into wine. And there was a certain royal official whose son lay sick at Capernaum. When this man heard that Jesus had arrived in Galilee from Judea, he went to see him and begged him to come and heal his son, who was close to death.* John 4:46-47

And finally, Cana is known as the hometown of one of the disciples, Nathanael, also known as Bartholomew.

*Afterward Jesus appeared again to his disciples, by the Sea of Tiberias. It happened this way: Simon Peter, Thomas (called Didymus), Nathanael from Cana in Galilee, the sons of Zebedee, and two other disciples were together. "I'm going out to fish," Simon Peter told them, and they said, "We'll go with you." So they went out and got into the boat, but that night they caught nothing.* John 21:1-3

---

**POINTS FROM THE PASTOR**

This first miraculous act at the beginning of Jesus' ministry, to me, exemplifies Isaiah 55:8, which reads: "For My thoughts are not your thoughts, neither are your ways my ways," declares the Lord. If you and I were kicking off a ministry, we'd probably want to start with a bang; however, Jesus' ministry began with a quiet act of kindness. Back then, weddings took place on the third day of the week and lasted for seven days. (And you thought today's weddings were expensive!) Running out of food or wine would have caused embarrassment to the family. Seeing their need, Jesus quietly stepped in to help. Don't let that slip past you unnoticed. His first miracle wasn't flashy or spectacular; there was no parting of the Red Sea or raising the dead. Instead, He launched His ministry by simply helping an average family with a pressing need. There is no question that this miracle demonstrates Christ's supernatural power and authority; but perhaps more important, it reveals His tender mercy toward us.

Next, we see the story of the official beseeching Jesus to heal his child. It's reasonable to assume that, in a town the size of Cana, word got around about what Jesus had done at the wedding. Who knows, maybe the royal official was just desperate enough to believe the small-town rumors and ask for the Lord's help. We don't know for sure why this man went to Jesus. What we do know for sure is that Jesus healed that little boy even though he was miles away in another city, and that is simply miraculous.[5]

## NAZARETH

*So he got up, took the child and his mother and went to the land of Israel. But when he heard that Archelaus was reigning in Judea in place of his father Herod, he was afraid to go there. Having been warned in a dream, he withdrew to the district of Galilee, and he went and lived in a town called Nazareth. So was fulfilled what was said through the prophets: "He will be called a Nazarene."* Matthew 2:21-23

Very little is known about Nazareth from ancient sources. It was just a small agricultural village that fell to Zebulun's lot when boundaries were being established. Then around 700 BC, the Assyrians conquered the area and the Jews were taken off into captivity. Gentiles settled so heavily in the region that Isaiah described it as "the Galilee of the Gentiles":

*...In the past he humbled the land of Zebulun and the land of Naphtali, but in the future he will honor Galilee of the Gentiles...* Isaiah 9:1

It's the rest of the prophecy, found in verses 2-9, that most of us know from Christmas services or Handel's Messiah, "For unto us a child is born..." that explains how the region would be honored one day. Can you imagine anything less likely than this insignificant little town becoming the hometown of the coming Messiah?

God began to set the stage around 100 BC when John Hyrcanus, as part of the Hasmonean conquest, opened up the way for Jews to begin to return from Persia and Babylon. It is likely that the whole line of David from the exiled land of Judah settled around Nazareth. Hyrcanus gave the Gentile occupiers two simple choices: convert to Judaism or leave. He was so successful that, by Jesus' day, most in Galilee were Jewish.

Modern Nazareth today seen from Mt. Tabor          *Photo: Todd Bolen*

Archaeological research suggests that, at the time of Jesus, the population of Nazareth was about 120 to 150, which meant a lot of gossip and very little privacy. Most likely everyone knew Mary and Joseph's story, though I doubt any of them believed it. Would you believe a young girl who came to you and said she had been impregnated by the Holy Spirit (Matthew 1:18-20)? Nonetheless, the story is true and, just as Isaiah had prophesied, this would be Christ's hometown. He grew up here, learned carpentry skills here, and around the age of 30, began His ministry here.

Sometime between 300 and 500 AD, a Byzantine church was built over the place where it is believed that the angel Gabriel announced the birth of Jesus to the Virgin Mary. In 1966, the Roman Catholic Church began constructing the Basilica of the Annunciation over these remains, and today it is the largest basilica in the Middle East.

The Greek Orthodox Church nearby is built over the town's water source.

## NAZARETH IN THE BIBLE

The angel Gabriel appeared to Mary and later to Joseph in Nazareth. Mary was pregnant here in this town—she may have given birth in Bethlehem, but all the scandal of her pregnancy would have been whispered about here. After a side trip to Bethlehem and then Egypt, Joseph and Mary returned and raised their family in this tightly-knit, remote, little village.

Near the beginning of His ministry, Jesus preached in His hometown synagogue and this small group of people who should have known Him best became so angry that they tried to throw Him off a cliff. Later in His ministry, Jesus returned to Nazareth, this time with His disciples (Matthew 13:54-58; Mark 6:1-6). Mark says the people were astonished by His wisdom and knew about the miracles that He had performed, but sadly, instead of receiving Him they "took offense."

POINTS FROM THE PASTOR

When arriving in Nazareth, you will be moved emotionally by the fact that you are driving through the town where Jesus actually lived. Though there are many things that have changed over the past 2,000 years, there's one particular site you need to insist your tour guide take you. Outside of town is a steep cliff from which the crowds once tried to throw Jesus (see Luke 4:29). Usually, tour buses will arrive at this site late in the day and travelers are too tired to even get off the bus. Don't settle for staying on the bus. Try to make your way up the snake path to the top of the cliff, so that you can experience this moment firsthand.

There is little doubt in my mind that if you had grown up in Nazareth, you would have climbed this cliff many times—because there's not a lot to do in a small village like this one! Certainly every child in Nazareth would have taken time to ascend the cliffs for an afternoon of fun and play. I am fully convinced that Jesus, too, must have climbed this precipice many times. With this in mind, open your Bible and read Luke 4:14-30. [6]

## SEPPHORIS

*"Isn't this the carpenter? Isn't this Mary's son and the brother of James, Joseph, Judas and Simon? Aren't his sisters here with us?" And they took offense at him.* Mark 6:3

Sepphoris, also known as Zipporis, is the traditional birthplace of Mary and is located in the center of Galilee. The area is surrounded by olive groves, pomegranate trees, grape vines, and fig trees—items often mentioned on the pages of the Bible. Though Jesus' hometown, Nazareth, is located just four miles to the south, Sepphoris is not mentioned in the New Testament.

Olive grove                                              *Photo: Steve Beaumont*

This site was known as "the jewel of the Galilee." As one of the capital cities of Galilee, it was a wealthy trading center. Historian Josephus called Sepphoris "the ornament of all Galilee," describing it as an exceptionally strong fortress. Herod Antipas chose this site in 4 BC as the capital of his government. The people of Sepphoris were so influenced by Rome that during the Jewish Revolt they supported Vespasian, the Roman emperor whose son would later destroy the Second Temple. They surrendered to the Romans to save their city from destruction and even minted coins in honor of Vespasian calling him the "peacemaker."

Sepphoris has been rightly called "The Forgotten City." Although commentaries and geography texts give attention to nearby Nazareth and Cana, Sepphoris is usually ignored. Though not mentioned in

Scripture, it was very influential in the region where Jesus lived and ministered.

The city was "perched like a bird" on a 400-foot hill overlooking the Bet Netofa Valley. Its Hebrew name, Zippori, or "bird," refers to its lofty location and panoramic views of Lower Galilee, including Cana and Nazareth.

Sepphoris was located about midway between the Mediterranean coast and the Sea of Galilee, and was situated on the well-traveled highway that connected the Mediterranean port of Ptolemais to the Sea of Galilee.

The highlight of the city is a 4,000-seat amphitheater, built into the eastern side of the hill probably while Jesus was a teenager. Its stage was 156 feet wide and 27 feet from front to back.

In one large building there are many mosaic floors, including the Nile mosaic in the largest room. This mosaic shows the Pharos lighthouse of Alexandria, which was one of the Seven Wonders of the Ancient World.

At the summit near the theater is a large dining room floor, which dates from around 300 AD. The building included a central triclinium, or formal dining room, with a mosaic made up of 1.5 million stones of 28 colors. The beautiful woman in the mosaic is nicknamed the "Mona Lisa of the Galilee."

## Sepphoris in the Bible

Again, although Sepphoris is not mentioned in the Bible, the importance of this city for believers is the fact that it was just four miles from Nazareth. During Jesus' early years, Herod Antipas was restoring, developing, and fortifying Sepphoris. It served as his principle residence and the administrative center of Galilee until he built Tiberias in 18-20 AD.

Also, according to tradition, Mary's parents, Joachim and Anna, lived in Sepphoris. If true, this busy trading center was Mary's hometown. Who knows, maybe Joseph, a young craftsman from Nazareth, met Mary while working in the city. Later, as Jesus was growing up, his grandparents would live just one hour away. It's safe to conclude that

Jesus would have been familiar with this town.

Aerial view of Sepphoris                                    *Photo: Todd Bolen*

Both Jesus and his father, Joseph, were known as carpenters (Matthew 13:55; Mark 6:3). We tend to think of a carpenter as someone who only works with wood; however, the Greek word for carpenter is actually tekton, which means "builder" and is often translated as "carpenter." To be a builder involved also being a stonecutter. Thus, Jesus was probably skilled in both wood and stone. Now, with Nazareth being such a small village, it would have had few construction projects for skilled builders. But with major construction, much of it in stone, happening just four miles away (or a one-hour walk), it's very probable that Jesus would have spent a lot of time working in Sepphoris.

**POINTS FROM THE PASTOR**

We don't know for sure, but there are hints that Jesus was well acquainted with Greek/Roman culture of the city. For instance, Jesus used the word hypocrite in his teachings (Matthew 6:2-16; 7:5; 15:7; 22:18; 23:13-29; 24:51; Mark 7:6; Luke 6:42; 12:56; 13:15). The word hypocrite is a Greek word taken from the theater world, which meant "stage actor." When you see the 4,500-seat theater in Sepphoris, just four miles from Jesus' hometown, you just have a feeling that Jesus would have been in this town many times. Isn't it inspiring to walk where Jesus walked?[7]

JEZREEL VALLEY / LOWER GALILEE

*Top:* Aerial view Mt. Tabor. *Photo: Todd Bolen*

*Middle:* Nazareth cliffs looking over Jezreel Valley. *Photo: Steve Beaumont*

*Above left:* Megiddo walkway. *Photo: Todd Bolen*

*Above right:* Adandoned roadside tomb along road to Megiddo. *Photo: Dudley Rutherford*

*Right:* Stairwell to Megiddo well system. *Photo: Todd Bolen*

# JOURNAL: JEZREEL VALLEY / LOWER GALILEE

# JOURNAL: JEZREEL VALLEY / LOWER GALILEE

---

**Fact Finder**: *In what town did Jesus live after he left Nazareth? (a) Jerusalem  (b) Tiberias (c) Bethsaida (d) Capernaum* Matthew 4:13

# JOURNAL: JEZREEL VALLEY / LOWER GALILEE

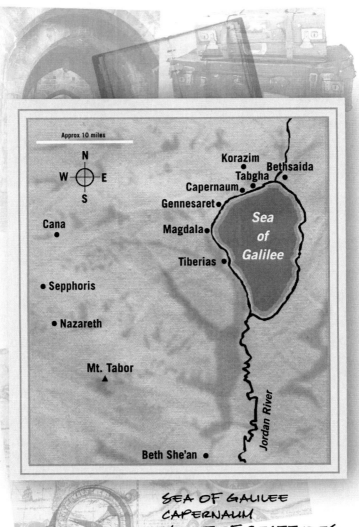

SEA OF GALILEE
CAPERNAUM
MOUNT OF BEATITUDES
TABGHA
THE JESUS BOAT

# Chapter 4: Galilee

## Sea of Galilee

*As Jesus walked beside the Sea of Galilee, he saw Simon and his brother Andrew casting a net into the lake, for they were fishermen. "Come, follow me," Jesus said, "and I will make you fishers of men." At once they left their nets and followed him.* Mark 1:16-18

Flavius Josephus, a Roman historian, sketched out the ancient boundaries of Galilee as follows: Akko (Acre) and Mount Carmel to the west, Samaria to the south, the Jordan River and the Sea of Galilee to the east, and to the north roughly the same border that exists today between Israel and Lebanon. The total region of Galilee is about 50 miles long, north to south, and 30 miles wide, east to west.

The largest body of water in Galilee is hard to miss. At 13 miles long, 7.5 miles wide, and only 150 feet at its deepest point, the Sea of Galilee—more properly designated as a lake—is one of the largest bodies of fresh water in the Middle East. It is fed by the Jordan River, rainfall, and springs on the northern side. (The Jordan River, by the way, flows the entire length of Israel and connects the Sea of Galilee in the north to the Dead Sea in the south. You can read more about the Jordan River in Chapter 6.) The rabbis have said of the Sea of Galilee, "Although God has created seven seas, yet He has chosen this one as His special delight." [1]

Galilee was composed of two sections: Upper and Lower Galilee. Draw a line from Akko to the Sea of Galilee on a map and you get a pretty good idea of where the division between Upper and Lower falls. Nazareth is located in Lower Galilee. Armageddon is located west, just across the valley from Nazareth.

## Sea of Galilee in the Bible

The Sea of Galilee is mentioned in the Bible by three other names:

1. The Sea of Kinneret (or Chinnereth), from its harp-like shape
2. The Sea of Tiberias
3. The Lake of Gennesaret

Nazareth, Mt. Tabor, Capernaum, Cana, and the Sea of Galilee are all in this one region. Much of Jesus' life was spent here. Thus, much of His ministry occurred here as well. As we go from site to site, try to remember that in Galilee you are walking where Jesus walked more than any other place in Israel—the thought alone is enough to knock your sandals off!

In those days, there was a ribbon of settlements and villages encircling the lake and plenty of trade and ferrying by boat. The Gospels of Mark 1:14-20, Matthew 4:18-22, and Luke 5:1-11 describe how Jesus recruited Simon, Andrew, James, and John from the shores of Galilee. Jesus delivered the Sermon on the Mount from a hill overlooking this lake, and many of His miracles were performed here including walking on water, calming a storm, and feeding 5,000 people in Tabgha.

Many famous sites are located around the lake, including Capernaum, home to at least five of the 12 disciples. The Church of the Beatitudes is said to mark where the Sermon on the Mount was preached and the Church of the Multiplication is said to mark the site where Jesus fed 5,000 followers from five loaves of bread and two fish. The nearby lakeside town of Migdal is the hometown of Mary Magdalene.

Of all the places in Israel, many people come away saying that the Sea of Galilee is their favorite part of the tour. There are a couple of reasons for this. First, this is where Jesus spent most of His time in ministry; almost all His teachings and miracles were conducted somewhere near this body of water. Second, it is the least commercialized of the towns in Israel and remains basically the same as it was in Jesus' day. As you take a boat ride across the Sea of Galilee, you truly get a sense for what our Lord felt and experienced.

Typically, I enjoy some leisure time around the lake and imagine Jesus walking on the water, bidding Peter to come. I imagine our

Lord instructing Peter and his men to cast their nets over the side of the boat, bringing up so many fish that their nets began to break and the boat began to sink. If you spend much time on the Sea of Galilee, you will notice that the weather can change quite rapidly and how quickly a storm can brew, and you will be able to fathom why Jesus suddenly had to rebuke the wind and the waves saying, "Quiet, be still! (Mark 4:39)"

It was in this region, and for three-and-a-half years, that Jesus discipled the Twelve and instilled within them the lessons and lifestyle of the Kingdom of God. Wouldn't it have been wonderful to have spent several years around this lake with Christ mentoring you and embedding in you the great urgency to take the Gospel into the whole world (Matthew 28:18-20)?[2]

## CAPERNAUM

*When Jesus heard that John had been put in prison, he returned to Galilee. Leaving Nazareth, he went and lived in Capernaum, which was by the lake in the area of Zebulun and Naphtali—to fulfill what was said through the prophet Isaiah: "Land of Zebulun and land of Naphtali, the way to the sea, along the Jordan, Galilee of the Gentiles – the people living in darkness have seen a great light; on those living in the land of the shadow of death a light has dawned." From that time on Jesus began to preach, "Repent, for the kingdom of heaven is near."* Matthew 4:12-17

Capernaum was a settlement on the north shore of the Sea of Galilee. It was near a main highway that connected Galilee to Damascus. The site is a ruin today but was inhabited from 150 BC to about 750 AD.

Capernaum is mentioned throughout the four Gospels. Luke cites it as the home of Peter, Andrew, James, John, and Matthew, the tax collector. Matthew 4:13 says that Jesus Himself lived there for a time and Mark 1:21 says He taught in the synagogue.

In Capernaum today you can find the beautiful remains of an ancient synagogue. The synagogue at Capernaum is not the one where Jesus preached, but it was probably built upon the footing and foundation of the 1st century synagogue. The recent discovery of coins in the mortar dates this reconstructed synagogue somewhere between the

4th and 5th century AD. Also in Capernaum you will find a house that some claim originally belonged to Simon Peter.

> The house of St. Peter, often mentioned by the Gospels in relation to the activity of Jesus in Capernaum, and recorded later on by pilgrims, was rediscovered in 1968 under the foundations of the octagonal church some 30 meters south of the synagogue. In the second half of the 5th century AD an octagonal church was built upon the house of St. Peter and remained in use until the 7th century AD. Stanislao Loffreda, Recovering Capernaum

Just north of the synagogue is a Roman milestone from the time of Hadrian that was discovered in 1975. Other items of interest at Capernaum include an oil press, a flourmill, and a wine press.

Capernaum olive oil press and synagogue today                    *Photos: Todd Bolen*

## Capernaum in the Bible

Capernaum was the epicenter of Jesus' ministry and miracles. It's hard to comprehend how many of His miracles happened here without looking at the biblical text. The following is only a partial list:

### Jesus Begins to Preach

*When Jesus heard that John had been put in prison, he returned to Galilee. Leaving Nazareth, he went and lived in Capernaum, which was by the lake in the area of Zebulun and Naphtali—to fulfill what was said through the prophet Isaiah: "Land of Zebulun and land of Naphtali, the way to the sea, along the Jordan, Galilee of the Gentiles—the people living in darkness have seen a great light; on those living in the land of the shadow of death a light has dawned." From that time on Jesus began to preach, "Repent, for the kingdom of heaven is near."* Matthew 4:12-17

## The Calling of the First Disciples

*As Jesus was walking beside the Sea of Galilee, he saw two brothers, Simon called Peter and his brother Andrew. They were casting a net into the lake, for they were fishermen. "Come, follow me," Jesus said, "and I will make you fishers of men." At once they left their nets and followed him. Going on from there, he saw two other brothers, James son of Zebedee and his brother John. They were in a boat with their father Zebedee, preparing their nets. Jesus called them, and immediately they left the boat and their father and followed him.* Matthew 4:18-22

## Jesus Heals the Sick

*Jesus went throughout Galilee, teaching in their synagogues, preaching the good news of the kingdom, and healing every disease and sickness among the people. News about him spread all over Syria, and people brought to him all who were ill with various diseases, those suffering severe pain, the demon-possessed, those having seizures, and the paralyzed, and he healed them. Large crowds from Galilee, the Decapolis, Jerusalem, Judea and the region across the Jordan followed him.* Matthew 4:23-25

## Jesus Calms the Storm

*Then he got into the boat and his disciples followed him. Without warning, a furious storm came up on the lake, so that the waves swept over the boat. But Jesus was sleeping. The disciples went and woke him, saying, "Lord, save us! We're going to drown!" He replied, "You of little faith, why are you so afraid?" Then he got up and rebuked the winds and the waves, and it was completely calm. The men were amazed and asked, "What kind of man is this? Even the winds and the waves obey him!"* Matthew 8:23-27

## Jesus Walks on the Water

*Immediately Jesus made the disciples get into the boat and go on ahead of him to the other side, while he dismissed the crowd. After he had dismissed them, he went up on a mountainside by himself to pray. When evening came, he was there alone, but the boat was already a considerable distance from land, buffeted by the waves because the wind was against it. During the fourth watch of the night Jesus went out to them, walking on the lake. When the disciples saw him walking on the lake, they were terrified. "It's a ghost," they said, and cried out in fear. But Jesus immediately said to them: "Take courage! It is I. Don't be afraid." "Lord, if it's you," Peter replied, "tell me to come to you on the water." "Come," he said. Then Peter got down out of the boat, walked on the water and came toward Jesus. But when he saw the wind, he was afraid and, beginning to sink, cried out, "Lord, save me!" Immediately Jesus reached out his hand and caught him. "You of little faith," he said, "why did you doubt?" And when they climbed into the boat, the wind died down. Then those who were in the boat worshiped him, saying, "Truly you are the Son of God." When they had crossed over, they landed at Gennesaret. And when the men of that place recognized Jesus, they sent word to all the surrounding country. People brought all their sick to him and begged him to let the sick just touch the edge of his cloak, and all who touched him were healed.* Matthew 14:22-36

## Jesus Heals Many

*When Jesus came into Peter's house, he saw Peter's mother-in-law lying in bed with a fever. He touched her hand and the fever left her, and she got up and began to wait on him. When evening came, many who were demon-possessed were brought to him, and he drove out the spirits with a word and healed all the sick. This was to fulfill what was spoken through the prophet Isaiah: "He took up our infirmities and carried our diseases."* Matthew 8:14-17

## The Faith of the Centurion

*When Jesus had entered Capernaum, a centurion came to him, asking for help. "Lord," he said, "my servant lies at home paralyzed and in terrible suffering." Jesus said to him, "I will go and heal him." The centurion replied, "Lord, I do not deserve to have you come under my roof. But just say the word, and my servant will be healed. For I myself am a man under authority, with soldiers under me. I tell this one, 'Go,' and he goes; and that one, 'Come,' and he comes. I say to my servant, 'Do this,' and he does it." When Jesus heard this, he was astonished and said to those following him, "I tell you the truth, I have not found anyone in Israel with such great faith. I say to you that many will come from the east and the west, and will take their places at the feast with Abraham, Isaac and Jacob in the kingdom of heaven. But the subjects of the kingdom will be thrown outside, into the darkness, where there will be weeping and gnashing of teeth." Then Jesus said to the centurion, "Go! It will be done just as you believed it would." And his servant was healed at that very hour.* Matthew 8:5-13

The people of Capernaum didn't just hear about the miracles of Jesus, they saw them firsthand. They heard His voice speak wisdom, truth, and mercy in their synagogue. They were there when He fed the 5000. They saw their friends and neighbors healed. Sadly, they ultimately made the same choice that the people of Nazareth, Jesus' hometown, made—refusing to repent and believe. Jesus describes these hardhearted eyewitnesses as being worse than Sodom! Listen to His words:

*"And you, Capernaum, will you be lifted up to the skies? No, you will go down to the depths. If the miracles that were performed in you had been performed in Sodom, it would have remained to this day. But I tell you that it will be more bearable for Sodom on the Day of Judgment than for you."*
Matthew 11:23-24

The town is still a ruin to this day.

During your visit, make sure you spend a little time looking at the 4th century synagogue in Capernaum. If you look on the  outside of the wall facing the west, you will see the foundation blocks of the 1st century synagogue. Look for a little sign that tells you this 4th century synagogue was built upon the foundation of the 1st century synagogue, and you can see that the original synagogue foundation was a much darker color of stone. It would have been inside this 1st century synagogue that Jesus gave the discourse in John 10 about the good shepherd and predicted that one day He would lay down His life for His sheep. Go inside the synagogue and read the following passage of Scripture:

*"I am the gate; whoever enters through me will be saved. He will come in and go out, and find pasture. The thief comes only to steal and kill and destroy; I have come that they may have life, and have it to the full.*

*"I am the good shepherd. The good shepherd lays down his life for the sheep. The hired hand is not the shepherd who owns the sheep. So when he sees the wolf coming, he abandons the sheep and runs away. Then the wolf attacks the flock and scatters it. The man runs away because he is a*

*hired hand and cares nothing for the sheep.*

*"I am the good shepherd; I know my sheep and my sheep know me—just as the Father knows me and I know the Father—and I lay down my life for the sheep. I have other sheep that are not of this sheep pen. I must bring them also. They too will listen to my voice, and there shall be one flock and one shepherd. The reason my Father loves me is that I lay down my life—only to take it up again. No one takes it from me, but I lay it down of my own accord. I have authority to lay it down and authority to take it up again. This command I received from my Father."* John 10:9-18. [3]

## MOUNT OF BEATITUDES

*Now when he saw the crowds, he went up on a mountainside and sat down. His disciples came to him, and he began to teach them saying: "Blessed are the poor in spirit, for theirs is the kingdom of heaven."* Matthew 5:1-3

The Sermon on the Mount is recorded in Matthew 5-7 and again in Luke 6, and it is regarded as one of the greatest pieces of literature ever spoken or written.[4] In this powerful discourse, Jesus Christ delivers important and practical steps for godly living—touching on such topics as our evangelistic duty as believers, the true fulfillment of the law, murder and anger, adultery and divorce, swearing oaths, forgiveness and love, charity, prayer that is pleasing to God, true wealth, worry, and judging others. Surely, Christ's Sermon on the Mount cut to the heart of Jesus' followers as they listened, and it should do the same for us today.

Scripture gives no indication of the exact location of this event, but the Byzantines built a church to commemorate it on the northern slopes overlooking the Sea of Galilee.

Once known as Mt. Eremos, this hill is located between Capernaum and Tabgha and is just above the "Cove of the Sower." We don't know for certain that this is where Jesus gave the Sermon on the Mount, which includes the Beatitudes, but it's a logical choice. This spacious hillside provides plenty of room for crowds to gather. In fact, 100,000 Catholics came here to observe mass in March of 2000 when Pope John Paul visited.

The Franciscan Sisters built a Catholic chapel at the top of the mountain in 1939. In front of the church, notice the symbols on the pavement that represent justice, prudence, fortitude, charity, faith, and temperance. Inside the church hangs the cloak from Pope Paul VI's visit in 1964.

Photo: Todd Bolen

Once you've taken a look around, find a quiet spot somewhere on the hillside and read the Beatitudes below. If you have time, open your Bible and read the entirety of the Sermon on the Mount in Matthew chapters 5 through 7. Try to imagine what it must have been like to hear these words for the very first time. Which words would have pricked you, confused you, or comforted you as you sat in the hot sun surrounded by multitudes of people? Let the truth of these words sink in as if Jesus had just spoken them for the first time:

## THE BEATITUDES

*"Blessed are the poor in spirit, for theirs is the kingdom of heaven. Blessed are those who mourn, for they will be comforted. Blessed are the meek, for they will inherit the earth. Blessed are those who hunger and thirst for righteousness, for they will be filled. Blessed are the merciful, for they will be shown mercy. Blessed are the pure in heart, for they will see God. Blessed are the peacemakers, for they will be called sons of God. Blessed are those who are persecuted because of righteousness, for theirs is the kingdom of heaven."*

*"Blessed are you when people insult you, persecute you and falsely say all kinds of evil against you because of me. Rejoice and be glad, because great is your reward in heaven, for in the same way they persecuted the prophets who were before you."* Matthew 5:3-12[5]

## TABGHA

*And he directed the people to sit down on the grass. Taking the five loaves and the two fish and looking up to heaven, he gave thanks and broke the loaves. Then he gave them to the disciples, and the disciples gave them to the people. They all ate and were satisfied, and the disciples picked up twelve basketfuls of broken pieces that were left over. The number of those who ate was about five thousand men, besides women and children.* Matthew 14:19-21

Two miles west of Capernaum is what Josephus referred to as the "well of Capernaum." No doubt, this was a popular fishing spot of the locals because of its famous "seven springs." Heptapegon (the name was eventually corrupted to Tabgha) is the traditional location for several events in Jesus' ministry. The seven springs that emerged at Tabgha (today only six have been discovered) produced water warmer than that of the Sea of Galilee. This set off a sort of biological domino effect, because the warm water brought algae, the algae brought fish, and the fish brought fishermen.

By 350 AD, pilgrims were coming to this site in the belief that this is where Jesus performed the miracle of the loaves and fishes. Eventually, a chapel was built. A pilgrim by the name of Egeria visited Tabgha around 380 AD and described what she saw.

> By the sea is a grassy field with plenty of hay and many palm trees. By them are seven springs (heptapegon), each flowing strongly. And this is the field where the Lord fed the people with the five loaves and two fishes. In fact the stone on which the Lord placed the bread has now been made into an altar. People who go there take away small pieces of the stone to bring them prosperity, and they are very effective. Travels of Egeria

Tabgha mosaic floor and church interior      *Photos: Todd Bolen*

The original chapel was enlarged around 480 AD and this is when the mosaic floors were added. The church was destroyed around 685 AD probably during Arab conquests. Over time silt and stone covered what was left of the church, and for about 1200 years these floors were forgotten. Then, in 1932, they were rediscovered. A protective cover was built over the site and in 1982 the modern church that exists today was built. The builders faithfully reconstructed the church according to its original design and the mosaic floors were restored. Take time to notice the basket of bread flanked by two fish.

## TABGHA IN THE BIBLE

Tabgha is the traditional location for the calling of the disciples. It is believed that here Jesus walked along the shore and called out to Simon Peter and Andrew who were casting their nets into the lake. Walking along, Jesus saw two other brothers, James and John who were preparing their nets with their father Zebedee. Jesus called these men to follow Him, promising that He would make them "fishers of men." Without hesitation, they left their nets and followed Him (Mark 1:16-20).

Tabgha's well-known mosaics commemorate Jesus' miraculous feeding of 5,000 from five loaves of bread and two fish.

*When Jesus heard what had happened, he withdrew by boat privately to a solitary place. Hearing of this, the crowds followed him on foot from the towns. When Jesus landed and saw a large crowd, he had compassion on them and healed their sick. As evening approached, the disciples came to him and said, "This is a remote place, and it's already getting late. Send the crowds away, so they can go to the villages and buy themselves some food." Jesus replied, "They do not need to go away. You give them something to eat." "We have here only five loaves of bread and two fish," they answered. "Bring them here to me," he said. And he directed the people to sit down on the grass. Taking the five loaves and the two fish and looking up to heaven, he gave thanks and broke the loaves. Then he gave them to the disciples, and the disciples gave them to the people. They all ate and were satisfied, and the disciples picked up twelve basketfuls of broken pieces that were left over. The number of those who ate was about five thousand men, besides women and children.* Matthew 14:13-21

Church history says that Jesus appeared in this location after His resurrection and that it is where the events of John 21 took place:

*Afterward Jesus appeared again to his disciples, by the Sea of Tiberias. It happened this way: Simon Peter, Thomas (called Didymus), Nathanael from Cana in Galilee, the sons of Zebedee, and two other disciples were together. "I'm going out to fish," Simon Peter told them, and they said, "We'll go with you." So they went out and got into the boat, but that night they caught nothing. Early in the morning, Jesus stood on the shore, but the disciples did not realize that it was Jesus. He called out to them, "Friends, haven't you any fish?" "No," they answered. He said, "Throw your net on the right side of the boat and you will find some." When they did, they were unable to haul the net in because of the large number of fish. Then the disciple whom Jesus loved said to Peter, "It is the Lord!" As soon as Simon Peter heard him say, "It is the Lord," he wrapped his outer garment around him (for he had taken it off) and jumped into the water. The other disciples followed in the boat, towing the net full of fish, for they were not far from shore, about a hundred yards. When they landed, they saw a fire of burning coals there with fish on it, and some bread. Jesus said to them, "Bring some of the fish you have just caught." Simon Peter climbed aboard and dragged the net ashore. It was full of large fish, 153, but even with so many the net was not torn. Jesus said to them, "Come and have breakfast." None of the disciples dared ask him, "Who are you?" They knew it was the Lord. Jesus came, took the bread and gave it to them, and did the same with the fish. This was now the third time Jesus appeared to his disciples after he was raised from the dead.* John 21:1-14[6]

## THE JESUS BOAT

*Going on from there, he saw two other brothers, James son of Zebedee and his brother John. They were in a boat with their father Zebedee, preparing their nets. Jesus called them, and immediately they left the boat and their father and followed him.* Matthew 4:21-22

The Sea of Galilee Boat, or the Jesus Boat, does not get its name from any personal association with Jesus, but from the fact that it is an ancient fishing boat from the time of Jesus (1st century AD). The boat, found in 1986, is

1st Century fishing boat        *Photo: Melissa Robles*

27 feet long and 7.5 feet wide. Moshe and Yuval Lufan, fishermen and amateur archaeologists from Kibbutz Ginnosar, discovered the boat when a prolonged drought caused the shoreline to recede. The two brothers stumbled upon the remains of the boat, which was partially buried in the newly exposed shore.

The brothers called the authorities who sent out a team of archaeologists to investigate. Realizing that the remains of the boat were of tremendous historical importance to Jews and Christians alike, a secret archaeological dig was undertaken by members of the Kibbutz Ginosar, the Israel Antiquities Authority, and numerous volunteers.

Like the proverbial rock and a hard place, the team was caught between two conflicting needs: caution and speed. One heavy rainfall could have ended all attempts to raise this boat, but if they had moved too quickly, this 2000-year-old artifact could have fallen apart. To make matters worse, a rumor spread that the boat was full of gold, so the site of the dig had to be guarded day and night.

Despite the obstacles, the team had the boat out in just 12 days. It was then submerged in a chemical bath for seven years before it could be displayed in the Yigal Allon Museum in Kibbutz Ginosar.

The boat has been dated to 40 BC (plus or minus 80 years) based on radiocarbon dating, and 50 BC to 50 AD based on the pottery (including a cooking pot and lamp) and nails found in the boat, as well as hull construction techniques. The evidence of repeated repairs done to the boat indicates that it was in use for several decades.

The Sea of Galilee Boat is historically important to Jews as an example of the type of boat used by their ancestors in the 1st century for both fishing and transportation across the lake. The boat is also important to Christians because this was the sort of boat used by Jesus and his disciples, several of whom were fishermen. Boats such as this played a large role in Jesus' life and ministry and are mentioned 50 times in the Gospels.[7]

---

Looking back on today's travels, I can't help but think that this was the lake where Jesus first called his disciples, saying, *"Come, follow me," Jesus said, "and I will make you fishers of men."* Mark 1:17

Whenever I'm near the Sea of Galilee, I always read this story and rejoice in the fact that as God called Simon Peter and Andrew to be "fishers of men," He has also called you and me to follow Him—and to joyfully accept this same assignment. In 2 Corinthians 5:18-21, the Apostle Paul explains that this assignment entails God entrusting believers with "the ministry of reconciliation" through Jesus Christ. We are now "ambassadors for Christ," pleading with the world on His behalf to be reconciled to God through repentance of sins and faith in the Father's one and only Son.

The only question that needs to be answered is this: Will we, like the early disciples, leave everything and follow Jesus? Will we begin to tell others about God's amazing grace? Perhaps this very moment, in the space provided below, you can write down the names of four or five people with whom you need to share Christ, and begin now to pray for their salvation.

_____

_____

_____

_____

_____

Make a commitment that when you return home, you will sit down with each of them and explain the importance of them putting their trust and faith in Jesus, and then joining you in becoming a "fisher of men." I pray that today's travel experience around the Sea of Galilee has motivated you to be a true follower of Jesus.

GALILEE

It's easy to imagine the sights and sounds that Jesus experienced while taking a pleasure cruise out onto the Sea of Galilee. *Photo: Dudley Rutherford*

*Top:* Capernaum synagogue from 4th century AD.
*Photo: Steve Beaumont*

*Middle left:* 4th century walls built over 1st century synagogue where Jesus taught.
*Photo: Todd Bolen*

*Above:* Excavated ruins of Capernaum homes at the time of Jesus. *Photo: Todd Bolen*

*Left:* Church on the site where Jesus delivered the Beatitudes in Matthew 5 through 7.
*Photo: Melissa Robles*

*Middle:* 4th century Capernaum columns still stand.
*Photo: Todd Bolen*

## JOURNAL: GALILEE

_____

_____

_____

_____

_____

_____

_____

_____

_____

_____

_____

_____

_____

_____

_____

_____

_____

_____

_____

_____

_____

_____

_____

_____

_____

**Fact Finder**_: What miracle did Jesus Christ do for man immediately after the Sermon on the Mount?_ Matthew 8:1-3

JOURNAL: GALILEE

TIBERIAS
KORAZIM/KORAZIN/CHORAZIN
MIGDAL/MAGDALA/MAGADAN
CAESAREA PHILIPPI

Tiberias sunrise          Photo: Dudley Rutherford

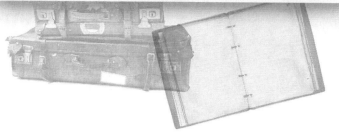

# CHAPTER 5: TIBERIAS

## TIBERIAS

*Then some boats from Tiberias landed near the place where the people had eaten the bread after the Lord had given thanks. Once the crowd realized that neither Jesus nor his disciples were there, they got into the boats and went to Capernaum in search of Jesus.* John 6:23-24

What appears to be a quaint little lake village has actually been in existence for more than 2,000 years. Since Roman times, Tiberias has been a vacation spot due to its 17 natural mineral hot springs. Herod Antipas (one of Herod the Great's three sons) built the city and named it in honor of the Roman emperor Tiberius. In Herod Antipas' time, the Jews refused to settle here; the presence of a cemetery made the site ritually unclean so Antipas settled Gentiles in Tiberias. He built a palace and made the city his new capital. Tiberias became so great that the Sea of Galilee soon came to be called the Sea of Tiberias. Like many cities throughout Israel, it found itself situated along several ancient trade routes leading to such places as Africa, Asia, and Iraq.

During the 1st Jewish-Roman War (66 AD) Josephus Flavius took control of the city and destroyed Herod's palace but stopped the city from being pillaged by his Jewish army. Most other cities in Palestine were razed once the Romans regained control, but Tiberias was spared because its inhabitants had remained loyal to Rome. After the fall of Jerusalem (70 AD) the southern Jewish population was expelled from Jerusalem and many migrated to Galilee. As a result, the city became more integrated with Jews and Gentiles.

In 145 AD, the Rabbi Shimon bar Yochai "cleansed the city of ritual impurity allowing Jews to settle in the city in numbers." Even the Sanhedrin, which had fled from Jerusalem during the Great Jewish Revolt against the Roman Empire, eventually settled in Tiberias around 150 AD. They would remain here until disbanding in the early Byzantine period around 300 AD. [1]

## Tiberias in the Bible

The Jewish locals in biblical times may have refused to live in this "unclean" city, but they would have been very aware of Herod's power and influence over their lives, especially since Tiberias was visible from Capernaum. One of Jesus' early followers was Joanna, wife of Chuza, Herod's steward (Luke 8:3). Chuza managed Herod's finances and royal estates, so it's reasonable to assume that Joanna and Chuza lived in Tiberias. It's almost certain that Herod had heard of Jesus' ministry; but they did not meet until Pilate, trying to pass the buck, sent Jesus to Herod's court (see Matthew 14:1-2; Mark 6:14-16; Luke 9:7-9; 23:6-12).

The day after Jesus fed the 5,000 at Bethsaida on the northeastern side of the lake, *other boats came from Tiberias, near the place where they ate bread after the Lord had given thanks...* (John 6:23). It's likely that these were people from Tiberias who followed Jesus, saw His miracles first-hand, and believed.

Then, after the Resurrection, Jesus appeared to the disciples:

*Afterward Jesus appeared again to his disciples, by the Sea of Tiberias. It happened this way: Simon Peter, Thomas (called Didymus), Nathanael from Cana in Galilee, the sons of Zebedee, and two other disciples were together. "I'm going out to fish," Simon Peter told them, and they said, "We'll go with you." So they went out and got into the boat, but that night they caught nothing. Early in the morning, Jesus stood on the shore, but the disciples did not realize that it was Jesus.* John 21:1-4

**POINTS FROM THE PASTOR**

You may notice a change in the climate right away when you arrive in Tiberias, which is situated 700 feet below sea level. With steep hills that shelter this city from the Mediterranean breeze that cools much of the Galilee, the temperature in Tiberias is much warmer. In fact, it's practically unbearable to endure in the summer heat and humidity. One traveler in the 1800s gave this harsh description of the town: "a picture of disgusting filth and frightful wretchedness." However, Tiberias is a flourishing resort today. Its streets are lined with palm trees and actually remind me of Hawaii and Southern California—two of my favorite places in the entire world. The Sea of Galilee glitters in the sunlight as if you are gazing upon a beautiful body of water at a tropical vacation spot, and you will observe remnants of the past (i.e. crusader castles and an ancient sea-wall) as well as lush gardens and greenery that hug its shore. Tiberias is an ideal, central location for touring Galilee.

The city is revered by the Jews as one of four holy cities of Judaism, along with Jerusalem, Hebron, and Safed. Although it didn't play a large role in early Christian history, Tiberias is regarded for the Jewish religious teachers who lived and worked here in the yeshivas (academies of biblical study) for 800 years after the Jews were banished from Jerusalem. Thus, significant contributions to the Mishnah and the Jerusalem Talmud—the authoritative writings on Jewish law—were made in Tiberias.

Rabbi Akiva and Moses Maimonides were among the most helpful interpreters of the Law, and their tombs here in Tiberias have become two of the most important Jewish pilgrimage sites. Akiva was a poor, semi-literate shepherd in the late 1st century/early 2nd century AD. Despite humble beginnings, he became one of Judaism's greatest scholars and one of the most essential contributors to the Mishnah. Maimonides was a 12th century philosopher and physician. He is often referred to as "the second Moses," and he explained the law in such helpful terms that he is still revered as an interpreter of the Jewish faith. There is a large metal structure over his burial place in the heart of the city, and some have said that it symbolizes a crown or a flame because Maimonides is so greatly respected in Jewish tradition.

It's important that Christians who desire to read the Old Testament intelligently are aware that the Law for the religious Jew is not merely rules and regulations, but the way of life that brings one closer to God. May it be the desire of each of our hearts to draw closer to the Lord during our journey through Israel and always.

## Korazim/Korazin/Chorazin

Korazim, also known as Korazin or Chorazin, was a small village two-and-a-half miles from Capernaum, situated on a large hill above the north shore of the Sea of Galilee, which was settled at the beginning of the 1st century AD. It is approximately 985 feet above the level of the lake.

We know a little about Korazim from Jewish writings and from history. The city and its surroundings are mentioned in Jewish Talmud (b. Menahot 85a). It is renowned for its very early harvest of grain, most likely due to an abundance of dark volcanic soil in the area. We learn from history that the city was destroyed, probably by an earthquake, in 363 AD and was rebuilt in the 5th century. In the 16th century, Jewish fishermen used to reside here.

Korazim synagogue and "Seat of Moses"                    *Photos: Todd Bolen*

Today, Korazim is an excavated ruin and the site of a National Archaeological Park. Extensive excavations and a survey were carried out here from 1962-1964 and were resumed from 1980-1987. This main settlement dates back to the 3rd and 4th centuries, and it resembles what you'd imagine Sodom and Gomorrah looked like after God destroyed them (Genesis 19:1-29). The ruins of Korazim are spread over an area of 25 acres, subdivided into five separate sections, with a large and impressive synagogue in the center.

The synagogue, like most of the other structures here, was built with black basalt stones (a volcanic rock found locally) and is the same type of synagogue found in Capernaum. Decorated with Jewish motifs, the ancient building also features a pair of stone lions—similar to a pair found in the synagogue at Kfar Bar'am in Northern Israel—floral decorations and other carvings such as images of wine making, a well-preserved Medusa, an armed soldier, and human and animal figures. Prominently displayed in the synagogue is the "Seat of Moses," to which Jesus may have been referring in Matthew 23:2. Sadly, these elements suggest the melding of Judaism with pagan beliefs and rituals of the time.

Near the ancient synagogue is a mikvah, or ritual bath, surrounded by public and residential buildings. Several olive millstones (used to extract olive oil) have been found in Korazim and suggest a dependence on the olive for economic purposes, like a number of other villages in northern, ancient Galilee. [2]

## Korazim in the Bible

This town's chief claim to fame is that Jesus cursed it (along with Bethsaida and Capernaum) because of its lack of repentance and belief—despite the miracles He performed there:

*Then Jesus began to denounce the cities in which most of his miracles had been performed, because they did not repent. "Woe to you, Korazin! Woe to you, Bethsaida! If the miracles that were performed in you had been performed in Tyre and Sidon, they would have repented long ago in sackcloth and ashes. But I tell you, it will be more bearable for Tyre and Sidon on the day of judgment than for you. And you, Capernaum, will you be lifted up to the skies? No, you will go down to the depths. If the miracles that were performed in you had been performed in Sodom, it would have remained to this day. But I tell you that it will be more bearable for Sodom on the day of judgment than for you."* Matthew 11:20-24

*"Woe to you, Korazin! Woe to you, Bethsaida! For if the miracles that were performed in you had been performed in Tyre and Sidon, they would have repented long ago, sitting in sackcloth and ashes. But it will be more bearable for Tyre and Sidon at the judgment than for you. And you, Capernaum, will you be lifted up to the skies? No, you will go down to the depths. "He who listens to you listens to me; he who rejects you rejects me; but he who rejects me rejects him who sent me."* Luke 10:13-16

**POINTS FROM THE PASTOR**

Throughout the Bible and throughout Jesus' teachings certain warnings have been issued, such as the destruction of Israel and Judah, the exile of the Jewish people (Deuteronomy 28:48-57; Jeremiah 25:9), and the destruction of the temple (Mark 13:1-2; Luke 21:5-6, 20-24). Whenever one walks within the ruins of a city of whose destruction has been prophesied, it should be a wakeup call for all of us that God will always be true to His Word. The Bible states clearly that a Day of Judgment is coming for all who do not accept Jesus Christ (Isaiah 34:1-4; Matthew 11:21-24; 12:35-37; 24:36-51; Mark 16:16; Romans 2:5; 1 Thessalonians 5:1-11; 2 Peter 3:7).

If you're visiting Korazim, standing in the midst of absolute ruin, take heart in knowing that despite God's wrath against the prevalent wickedness and corruption in the world, He is also just and full of great mercy. One day God will indeed spare every person who turns from their sins and surrenders their life to Christ Jesus by faith (2 Chronicles 7:14; Joel 2:32; Matthew 24:13; John 3:16-17; Acts 2:20-22; Romans 10:9).[3]

**Fact Finder**: *How many demons were brought out of Mary Magdalene by Jesus?* Luke 8:2

## MIGDAL/MAGDALA/MAGADAN

*Mary Magdalene went to the disciples with the news: "I have seen the Lord!" And she told them that he had said these things to her.* John 20:18

Migdal was founded in 1910, but what makes this town so interesting is its connection to Magdala (sometimes called Magadan in Greek translations of the New Testament). Modern-day Migdal is thought to stand on the site where ancient Magdala once stood. Magdala, just a few miles from Tiberias, was a city that would have been well known to Jesus and His disciples. It's likely that the fishermen/ disciples often sailed to Magdala with their catch of fish. Here their fish were sold, salted, and shipped. The fishing

Magdala mosaic          *Photo: Todd Bolen*

catch of fish. Here their fish were sold, salted, and shipped. The fishing industry was such a large part of the city that its two other names were Tericheae (derived from the Greek word for "salted fish") and Magdala Nunayya or "Magdala of the fishes."

Before Herod built Tiberias, Magdala was the most important city on the lake. It had a hippodrome, a large population, and a reputation for immorality. Today, most know of Magdala because of one particular citizen who is mentioned in all four Gospels: Mary Magdalene. It's assumed that Mary Magdalene meant "Mary of Magdala" just as someone from Nazareth was called a Nazarene.

## Mary Magdalene in the Bible

Mary of Magdala, like many of us, was in pretty sad shape before meeting Jesus. Possessed by seven demons, she must have felt completely helpless and hopeless until the day the Lord cast out her demons (Luke 8:2). She never forgot who had saved her and she stayed close—joining with others, including the 12 disciples, who accompanied Jesus during His ministry (Luke 8:1-2). She stood with Mary, the mother of Jesus, at the foot of the cross (John 19:25), and she was the first human witness to His resurrection:

*Early on the first day of the week, while it was still dark, Mary Magdalene went to the tomb and saw that the stone had been removed from the entrance. So she came running to Simon Peter and the other disciple, the one Jesus loved, and said, "They have taken the Lord out of the tomb, and we don't know where they have put him!" So Peter and the other disciple started for the tomb. Both were running, but the other disciple outran Peter and reached the tomb first. He bent over and looked in at the strips of linen lying there but did not go in. Then Simon Peter came along behind him and went straight into the tomb. He saw the strips of linen lying there, as well as the cloth that had been wrapped around Jesus' head. The cloth was still lying in its place, separate from the linen. Finally the other disciple, who had reached the tomb first, also went inside. He saw and believed. (They still did not understand from Scripture that Jesus had to rise from the dead.) Then the disciples went back to where they were staying. Now Mary stood outside the tomb crying. As she wept, she bent over to look into the tomb and saw two angels in white, seated where Jesus' body had been, one at the head and the* *foot. They asked her, "Woman, why are you crying?" "They have taken my Lord away," she said, "and I don't know where they have put him." At this, she turned around and saw Jesus standing there, but she did not realize that it was Jesus. He asked her, "Woman, why are you crying? Who is it you are looking for?" Thinking he was the gardener, she said, "Sir, if you have carried him away, tell me where you have put him, and I will get him." Jesus said to her, "Mary." She turned toward him and cried out in Aramaic, "Rabboni!" (which means "Teacher"). Jesus said, "Do not hold on to me, for I have not yet ascended to the Father. Go instead to my brothers and tell them, 'I am ascending to my Father and your Father, to my God and your God.'" Mary Magdalene went to the disciples with the news: "I have seen the Lord!" And she told them that he had said these things to her.* John 20:1-18*

## Caesarea Philippi

*When Jesus came to the region of Caesarea Philippi, he asked his disciples, "Who do people say the Son of Man is?"* Matthew 16:13

The ancient Roman city of Caesarea Philippi is mentioned in Matthew, Mark, and Acts. Today, it is an uninhabited archaeological site. Located 25 miles north of the Sea of Galilee at the base of Mount Hermon, it is the home of one of the largest of the four springs that feed the Jordan River. The abundant water supply made the area very fertile and attractive for religious worship, and numerous temples were built here.

This city has had a long history of pagan worship—first, the Phoenician god Ba'al, then the Greek god Pan. A cave near Caesarea Philippi was said to be the birthplace of Pan, and a grotto shrine dedicated to him gave this site the name Paneas in early Roman times.

Caesarea Philippi, which translates "Philip's city of Caesar," was built by Herod's son Philip on a large plateau at the foot of Mount Hermon near the headwaters of the Jordan River. Herod built a temple dedicated to the Roman emperor Augustus here, but it was Philip who took the fresh water pools, fertile soil, and hilltop views and turned this place into one of the best resorts in Palestine. In a fit of modesty, he renamed it Caesarea Philippi after himself.

Caesarea Philippi rock niches and excavated ruins          *Photos: Melissa Robles*

Later, Herod Agrippa II (the grandson of Herod the Great) renamed the city Neronias to honor Emperor Nero, but after Nero committed suicide the name was changed back to Paneas. The area's modern name is Banias, an Arabic corruption of Panias.

## CAESAREA PHILIPPI IN THE BIBLE

It is possible that Jesus visited Caesarea Philippi since it is located so close to Galilee, Nazareth, and Capernaum. However, the Bible does not say specifically that He entered the city; just that He came to the region (Matthew 16:13).

Caesarea Philippi rests on the southwestern slope of Mount Hermon, which happens to be the tallest mountain in all of Israel at 9,232 feet above sea level and 11,000 feet above the level of the Jordan Valley. As mentioned in Chapter 3, there is some debate that the transfiguration in Matthew 17 may have taken place at Mount Hermon instead of Mount Tabor.

But without question, Caesarea Philippi is, at the very least, the backdrop to one of the most dramatic events in the New Testament when Jesus asked His disciples, *"Who do men say I am?"*

*When Jesus came to the region of Caesarea Philippi, he asked his disciples, "Who do people say the Son of Man is?" They replied, "Some say John the Baptist; others say Elijah; and still others, Jeremiah or one of the prophets." "But what about you?" he asked. "Who do you say I am?" Simon Peter* answered, *"You are the Christ, the Son of the living God." Jesus replied, "Blessed are you, Simon son of Jonah, for this was not revealed to you by man, but by my Father in heaven. And I tell you that you are Peter, and on this rock I will build my church, and the gates of Hades will not overcome it. I will give you the keys of the kingdom of heaven; whatever you bind on earth will be bound in heaven, and whatever you loose on earth will be loosed in heaven." Then he warned his disciples not to tell anyone that he was the Christ.* Matthew 16:13-20

---

**POINTS FROM THE PASTOR**

Caesarea Philippi is one of the most beautiful regions in all of Israel. The freshwater pools, lush trees, and temple ruins make it a favorite stop on this tour of the Holy Land. The bus ride to the city is 25 miles of winding roads north of the Sea of Galilee and  passes quite closely to the Syrian border and the base of the Golan Heights. Ask your guide to explain the importance of the Golan Heights in regards to Israel's security.

During your visit, it is important to note that the prevalence of false gods in this region made Jesus' question in Matthew 16 all the more compelling. *"Who do men say that I am?"* Simon Peter answered, *"You are the Christ, the Son of the living God,"* and Jesus responded emphatically by saying, *"I tell you that you are Peter, and on this rock I will build my church, and the gates of Hades will not overcome it."*

It was here in this setting that Jesus reveals that He is the Messiah. Peter was not the rock. The mountainous rock near or upon which this important conversation took place, was not the rock either. The rock is the object of Peter's confession, that Jesus Himself is the "Son of the Living God." Jesus is the rock of all ages and the chief cornerstone of the Church—a force that can never be destroyed or weakened by the gates of hell. Now is a good time to ask yourself how you would have answered Jesus' question. Who do you say the Son of Man is? Your confession (see Romans 10:9-10) is a matter of salvation.

CAESAREA PHILIPPI/ TIBERIAS

*Top:* Entry to Caesarea Philippi *Photo: Dudley Rutherford*
*Middle:* Caesarea Philippi aerial view *Photo: Todd Bolen*
*Above:* Boys at play in Tiberias *Photo: Dudley Rutherford*
*Right:* Boats moored in Tiberias *Photo: Steve Beaumont*

## JOURNAL: TIBERIAS

_____

_____

_____

_____

_____

_____

_____

_____

_____

_____

_____

_____

_____

_____

_____

_____

_____

_____

_____

_____

_____

_____

_____

_____

_____

_____

_____

_____

_____

_____

JOURNAL: TIBERIAS

JORDAN RIVER
BAPTISMAL SERVICE AT
    THE JORDAN RIVER
BETH SHE'AN
JERICHO
JERUSALEM INTRODUCED

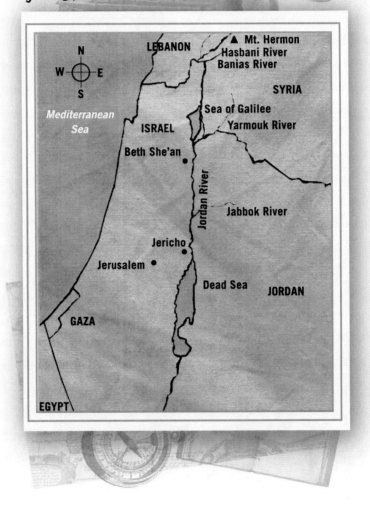

**Fact Finder**: *Saul initially was buried in Jabesh in Gilead after his body was recovered from Beth She'an. What Israelite king, who succeeded Saul, was responsible for Saul being reburied in Saul's tribal homeland of Benjamin? 2 Samuel 21:12*

# Chapter 6: Jordan River Valley

## Jordan River

*Then Jesus came from Galilee to the Jordan to be baptized by John. But John tried to deter him, saying, "I need to be baptized by you, and do you come to me?" Jesus replied, "Let it be so now; it is proper for us to do this to fulfill all righteousness." Then John consented. As soon as Jesus was baptized, he went up out of the water. At that moment heaven was opened, and he saw the Spirit of God descending like a dove and lighting on him. And a voice from heaven said, "This is my Son, whom I love; with him I am well pleased."*
Matthew 3:13-17

The Jordan River Valley is mentioned frequently in the Bible. In fact, it is mentioned about 175 times in the Old Testament and about 15 times in the New Testament. The name Jordan literally translates "the descender," which makes sense once you know a little about the valley.

The headwaters of the Jordan are at the base of Mt. Hermon, and, as mentioned in the previous section, four main streams feed the Jordan here: the Nahr Banias, the Nahr el Leddan, the Nahr Hasbani, and the Nahr Bareight. I'm going to go out on a limb here and guess that the word Nahr means river.

The Jordan River descends in a series of steps. The first is from Mt. Hermon to Lake Huleh—and it is a doozy, with a drop of more than 8,000 feet. Lake Huleh's altitude is about 1,000 feet above sea level. The river flows through Lake Huleh and continues on to the Sea of Galilee, which is 685 feet below sea level. From there it descends another 600 feet, emptying into the Dead Sea, which is 1,275 feet below sea level. That name, "the descender," makes a lot more sense now, doesn't it?

The river itself follows a winding, nearly 200-mile long course. In modern and in ancient times, it has been used as a natural boundary line. Up north it is used as a western boundary for the Golan Heights, and down south it divides Jordan and Israel. Sadly, it is also a bone of contention between Arabs and Jews today. In 1964, Israel began operating a dam, which diverted water from the Sea of Galilee. That same year Jordan constructed a channel to divert water from the Yarmouk River, a main tributary of the Jordan. Syria has also built reservoirs to catch the Yarmouk's waters. All of these changes have caused the Dead Sea—at the end of the water pipeline—to begin to dry up. In fact, the shallow southern end of the Dead Sea is now a salt flat.

Aerial view of Jordan river and salt crystals on edge of Dead Sea    *Photos: Todd Bolen*

## JORDAN RIVER IN THE BIBLE

The first mention of the Jordan is when Abraham and Lot parted company. *Lot looked up and saw that the whole plain of the Jordan was well watered, like the garden of the LORD... So Lot chose for himself the whole plain of the Jordan and set out toward the east. The two men parted company.* Genesis 13:10-11

Later, the Israelites would pass through the Jordan River on their way into the Promised Land. Notice how God bookends their time in the desert: Moses led them out of Egypt and God miraculously parted the Red Sea; then 40 years later, God re-enacts that same miracle for a new generation. When the priests carrying the Ark of the Covenant stepped into the water, God again miraculously holds back the water, allowing all the people to pass through on dry ground (Joshua 3).

Scripture cites two miracles the prophet Elisha performed at the Jordan River. He commanded the Syrian general, Naaman, to wash in the Jordan seven times to be healed of his leprosy. At first, Naaman rejected this directive, considering it foolish. When he finally obeyed, God healed him (2 Kings 5:10-14). Also, Elisha caused an iron axhead to float after it had fallen into the Jordan (2 Kings 6:1-7).

John the Baptist came out of the wilderness and began preaching and baptizing in the Jordan River area (Matthew 3:5-6; Mark 1:5; John 1:28; 3:26). John also baptized Jesus in the Jordan as He began His public ministry (Matthew 3:13; Mark 1:9; Luke 3:21-4:1).[1]

## Baptismal Service at the Jordan River

Baptisms in the Jordan River                    Photo: Melissa Robles

One of the highlights of a visit to the Holy Land is seeing the Jordan River, especially going to the area where people are allowed to be baptized. It's just south of the Sea of Galilee and in recent years has been updated with modern facilities along with a nice shopping area. If you are contemplating being baptized in the Jordan River, it's a must to understand the Scriptures concerning baptism. Try to spend some of your leisure time around the Sea of Galilee studying the following passages:

### Matthew 28:18-20
Jesus commands His disciples to go into the world baptizing and making disciples of other men and women.

### Acts 2:26-40
Three-thousand people respond to Peter's sermon on the Day of Pentecost by being baptized into the name of Jesus Christ. Pay careful attention to verse 38.

### Romans 6:3-5
Baptism symbolizes the actual death, burial, and resurrection of our Lord and Savior Jesus Christ.

Acts 8:26-40

The Ethiopian eunuch orders the chariot to stop so that he might be baptized after Philip teaches him about Jesus.

Acts 22:2-16

The Apostle Paul gives his testimony and concludes with the story of his baptism.

---

If you believe that Jesus is the Christ, the Son of the Living God, then you need to be baptized into the name of the Father, the Son and the Holy Spirit. "Why?" you might ask. Because the above-mentioned Scriptures teach us that being baptized is more than just a novel thing to do, it encompasses some heavy spiritual significance. In Matthew 28:18-20, we learn that Jesus commands every believer in Him to be baptized. In Acts 2:36-41, we see that at the inception of the early Church at Pentecost—a day marked by the falling of the Holy Spirit—Peter commands all of the believers to be baptized. In Romans 6:3-5, we see that we are declaring our faith and belief in the death, burial, and resurrection of Jesus through the act of baptism.

POINTS FROM THE PASTOR

In case you've never been baptized, your visit to the Jordan River might be an excellent place and time to fully surrender your life to the Lord. And to be baptized in the same river in which Jesus was baptized will truly knock your sandals off! Well, your sandals should already be off before you enter the water, but you know what I mean.

There are a few prerequisites—or things that must take place—before you are baptized:

1.) You must believe in your heart that Jesus is the Son of God. (John 3:16)
2.) You must repent, which means to decide to walk towards God instead of walking away from God. (Luke 13:3)
3.) You must confess or acknowledge that Jesus is Lord, King, and Ruler of your life! (Romans 10:9-10)

If you can boldly proclaim these three convictions in your life, then run to the water's edge! But be forewarned—if you do surrender fully to Christ and are baptized into His name, a celebration immediately begins in heaven because of the faith and trust you have placed in Him (Luke 15:7).

Note: Some people desire to recommit their lives to the Lord and be re-baptized during this spiritual pilgrimage. Although there is no scriptural precedence for being re-baptized, let 1 Peter 3:21 be your guide.

*...and this water symbolizes baptism that now saves you also—not the removal of dirt from the body but the pledge of a clear conscience toward God. It saves you by the resurrection of Jesus Christ,* 1 Peter 3:21

While every baptism service is special, one can't help but be emotionally moved either by witnessing or actually experiencing a baptism here along the bank of the Jordan River. The quiet solitude of nature is only interrupted by the expressing of faith towards the acceptance of Jesus Christ into the hearts of believers.

What are your thoughts at this particular time? Even if you were baptized many years ago, how has this simple ceremony of baptism changed your life?

_____

_____

_____

_____

_____

_____

_____

_____

_____

# Beth She'an

*The next day, when the Philistines came to strip the dead, they found Saul and his three sons fallen on Mount Gilboa. They cut off his head and stripped off his armor, and they sent messengers throughout the land of the Philistines to proclaim the news in the temple of their idols and among their people. They put his armor in the temple of the Ashtoreths and fastened his body to the wall of Beth Shan.* 1 Samuel 31:8-10

As we drive south from the Sea of Galilee and cross the Jordan River, we enter the Beth She'an Valley. Located 17 miles south of the Sea of Galilee, Beth She'an is situated at the strategic junction of the Harod and Jordan valleys. It is a small town with many names: Beth She'an (the actual Hebrew word is pronounced "bayth-she-awn"), Bet She'an, Beit She'an, Beth Shan (the abbreviated form), Beisan—and just to keep things interesting, Scythopolis. Besides having a long list of names, it has a long history that dates back to biblical times. According to the Talmud, "If the garden of Eden is in Israel, then its gate is in Bet She'an." Set between two valleys, it has fertile land and plenty of water. This explains why so many invaders have conquered and then settled here.

Today Beth She'an is best known for its spectacular archaeological excavations. The Bet She'an tel is about 262 feet tall, and 18 previous cities have been built on this site—one on top of the next. Picture a stack of pancakes and you have the general idea. In the 15th century BC, Beth She'an was listed among Thutmose III's conquests. The city was used as an Egyptian administrative center, and ruins from this time have been found. Egyptian stellae from the time of Seti I and Ramses II were also uncovered here and later moved to the Rockefeller Museum in Jerusalem.

The Egyptians were eventually conquered by the Canaanites, who controlled Beth She'an until the Philistines conquered them around the 11th century BC. It was during Philistine rule that Saul's body was hung from the wall of Beth She'an as mentioned in the above Scripture reference. Later, the city came under Jewish control with the conquests of King David. Ruins from this era have also been uncovered.

The city seemed to drop from the historical radar until around the

3rd century BC when Greco-Romans rebuilt and renamed the city "Scythopolis." Ruins from an 8,000-seat theater, a stone colonnade, basalt streets, and a one-and-a-half acre Roman thermae (bath house) can still be seen today. From the 4th to the 7th centuries AD, Byzantines ruled Beth She'an. Under their rule the city prospered and grew to its largest size—a population of 40,000. Many beautiful mosaics survived this period.

Beth She'an main street and bath house          *Photos: Dudley Rutherford*

In 634 AD, Muslims captured and renamed the city once again, this time, "Besian." The city fell into decline and much of the marble was carted off and crushed to make lime. Like taking a wrecking ball to a condemned building, an earthquake in 749 AD destroyed what was left of the city. It remained mostly abandoned for the next thousand years. The Swiss-German traveler, Johann Ludwig Burkhart, described Beth She'an in 1812 as "a village with 70 to 80 houses, whose residents are in a miserable state."

Beth She'an was put back on the map in 1921when the University of Pennsylvania began excavating. Then, nine seasons of excavations were conducted from 1989 to 1996 by the Institute of Archaeology at the Hebrew University of Jerusalem.

This is always one of the most impressive archaeological sites that one will visit while touring throughout all of Israel.

## Beth She'an in the Bible

Beth She'an was one of the ancient cities of the Decapolis mentioned in Mark 5:20 and Mark 7:31. Beth She'an and the surrounding towns were assigned to the tribe of Manasseh, but fearing the iron chariots of the Canaanite inhabitants, the Israelites failed to drive the Canaanites out of Beth She'an (Joshua 17:16-17).

But perhaps the most well-known biblical story involving the town is when Saul and his three sons died on Mount Gilboa; the Philistine victors carried their decapitated bodies to Beth She'an and hung them on the city wall to humiliate the Israelites. When the Israelites heard of this travesty, the men of Jabesh Gilead marched through the night (a distance of 12 miles) to recover the bodies of the king and his sons. They carried them back to Jabesh Gilead where they burned them and buried the ashes. You can read the story in 1 Samuel 31:1-13 on the following page.

Israel finally conquered Beth She'an during the reign of King Solomon, some four hundred years after Joshua's conquest of the area (1 Kings 4:12).[2]

---

**POINTS FROM THE PASTOR** Grab your hat and your sunblock because this archaeological site requires some time and walking—perhaps even some climbing. But when you think back over your trip to Israel, this will be one of the highlights of the entire tour. Stick close to your guide so that you don't miss any of the intriguing details about this city.

One of my favorite things to do in Beth She'an is to sit in the Roman theater and pose this question to my group: "Who here can sing—I mean, really sing?" Inevitably, someone in the group will have a great singing voice, so I instruct them to go down to the stage below and sing a special hymn like "Amazing Grace," "Shout to the Lord," or "I Surrender All," while the rest of us listen and enjoy. Be prepared to be moved by the incredible natural acoustics of the theater.

Beth She'an theater          *Photo: Melissa Robles*

Next, even though it may appear too difficult, make your way to the top of the tel by climbing the lengthy, man-made stairs to the right. It is a challenge, but the view of the city below—not just the physical fatigue from the climb—will take your breath away. So, you'd better double-tie your sandals, because you know what happens to them whenever you see all these awesome sites here in Israel! From the tel's crest, you will be able to look to the north to Mount Gilboa and into the Jezreel Valley to see where Gideon defeated the Midianites in Judges 7.

Finally, it is a strange thing to be in the very place where Saul's body was hung on the wall after he was beheaded by the Philistines. Have someone in your group read the two following passages aloud. This story took place about 1010 BC, a thousand years before Christ:

*Now the Philistines fought against Israel; the Israelites fled before them, and many fell slain on Mount Gilboa. The Philistines pressed hard after Saul and his sons, and they killed his sons Jonathan, Abinadab and Malki-Shua. The fighting grew fierce around Saul, and when the archers overtook him, they wounded him critically.*

*Saul said to his armor-bearer, "Draw your sword and run me through, or these uncircumcised fellows will come and run me through and abuse me."*

*But his armor-bearer was terrified and would not do it; so Saul took his own sword and fell on it. When the armor-bearer saw that Saul was dead, he too fell on his sword and died with him. So Saul and his three sons and his armor-bearer and all his men died together that same day.*

*When the Israelites along the valley and those across the Jordan saw that the Israelite army had fled and that Saul and his sons had died, they abandoned their towns and fled. And the Philistines came and occupied them.*

*The next day, when the Philistines came to strip the dead, they found Saul and his three sons fallen on Mount Gilboa. They cut off his head and stripped off his armor, and they sent messengers throughout the land of the Philistines to proclaim the news in the temple of their idols and among their people. They put his armor in the temple of the Ashtoreths and fastened his body to the wall of Beth Shan.*

*When the people of Jabesh Gilead heard of what the Philistines had done to Saul, all their valiant men journeyed through the night to Beth*

*Shan. They took down the bodies of Saul and his sons from the wall of Beth Shan and went to Jabesh, where they burned them. Then they took their bones and buried them under a tamarisk tree at Jabesh, and they fasted seven days.* 1 Samuel 31:1-13

Then, after the word of Saul's death was brought to David in Ziklag, David sings this lament in 2 Samuel 1:19-27:

*"Your glory, O Israel, lies slain on your heights.*
    *How the mighty have fallen!*

*"Tell it not in Gath,*
    *proclaim it not in the streets of Ashkelon,*
    *lest the daughters of the Philistines be glad,*
    *lest the daughters of the uncircumcised rejoice.*

*"O mountains of Gilboa,*
    *may you have neither dew nor rain,*
    *nor fields that yield offerings of grain.*
    *For there the shield of the mighty was defiled,*
    *the shield of Saul—no longer rubbed with oil.*

*From the blood of the slain,*
    *from the flesh of the mighty,*
    *the bow of Jonathan did not turn back,*
    *the sword of Saul did not return unsatisfied.*

*"Saul and Jonathan—*
    *in life they were loved and gracious,*
    *and in death they were not parted.*
    *They were swifter than eagles,*
    *they were stronger than lions.*

*"O daughters of Israel,*
    *weep for Saul,*
    *who clothed you in scarlet and finery,*
    *who adorned your garments with ornaments of gold.*

*"How the mighty have fallen in battle!*
    *Jonathan lies slain on your heights.*

*I grieve for you, Jonathan my brother;*
    *you were very dear to me.*

*Your love for me was wonderful,*
*more wonderful than that of women.*

*"How the mighty have fallen!*
*The weapons of war have perished!"*

## JERICHO

*Jesus entered Jericho and was passing through. A man was there by the name of Zacchaeus; he was a chief tax collector and was wealthy. He wanted to see who Jesus was, but being a short man he could not, because of the crowd. So he ran ahead and climbed a sycamore-fig tree to see him, since Jesus was coming that way. When Jesus reached the spot, he looked up and said to him, "Zacchaeus, come down immediately. I must stay at your house today." So he came down at once and welcomed him gladly.* Luke 19:1-6

The city of Jericho is located near the Jordan River in the West Bank of the Palestinian territories. At 825 feet below sea level, it is the lowest oasis and town in the world.[3] Jericho is also believed to be one of the oldest continuously inhabited cities on earth, occupied since approximately 3000 BC.

Uncovered Jericho Neolithic tower and ancient pool with steps          *Photos: Todd Bolen*

After Jerusalem, Jericho is the most excavated place in Israel. The Tel e-Sultan is the site of ancient Jericho. Little remains beyond a few piles of rocks that archaeologists say were once parts of towers, staircases, and other structures—the oldest of which date back to 10,000-9000 BC. In 1868, Charles Warren sank several shafts and concluded that nothing was to be found. However, he missed the Neolithic tower by just three feet. Later uncovered by the Kenyon excavation of 1952-1958, the Neolithic tower is thought to date back to 8000-7000 BC. On the basis of this and many other artifacts discovered here, archaeologists have claimed that Jericho is the "oldest city in the world."

Jericho sits between Mt. Nebo to the east, the Central Mountains to the west, and the Dead Sea to the south. In addition to these natural fortifications, Jericho is also rich in water—it is fed by the Jordan River (which is just four miles to the west) and by underground streams from the Central Mountains. Jericho stands like an island of green in a sea of barren desert. Its natural resources, central location, beauty, and natural defenses made Jericho ideal for trade—but also a target for invaders.

In the 8th century BC, the Assyrians invaded from the north, followed by the Babylonians. Jericho sat empty between 586 and 538 BC, but when Cyrus the Great conquered the Babylonians in 539 BC, he had Jericho rebuilt one mile to the southeast of the historic site and returned the Jews from exile. He also made the new Jericho an administrative center for his Persian empire.

Next, Jericho went from being an administrative center under Persian rule to serving as the private estate of Alexander the Great between 336 and 323 BC after his conquest of the region. During this period of Greek occupation, many forts were built to strengthen Jericho. One of these forts was later refortified by Herod the Great and renamed "Kypros" after his mother.

Herod initially leased Jericho from Cleopatra after Mark Antony gave it to her as a gift. After the couple's joint suicide in 30 BC, Octavian assumed control of the Roman Empire and gave Herod free rein over Jericho. Under Herod's rule, a hippodrome-theater was built to entertain his guests as well as new aqueducts to irrigate the land below the cliffs and to provide water for his winter palace.

First century AD Jericho is described in Strabo's *Geography* as "a plain surrounded by a kind of mountainous country, which in a way, slopes toward it like a theatre. Here is the Phoenicon, which is mixed also with all kinds of cultivated and fruitful trees, though it consists mostly of palm trees. It is 100 stadia in length and is everywhere watered with streams. Here also are the Palace and the Balsam Park."

The city has been destroyed and rebuilt many times. The Romans destroyed the old city in the 1st century. The Byzantines rebuilt the city on its present site. In 747 AD, an earthquake destroyed the city.

During the Crusades, both sides controlled Jericho at one point, but eventually Saladin, the sultan of Egypt and Syria, recaptured and held the city in the 12th century. Jericho was largely ignored and deserted for centuries afterward. (A quick word about Saladin, the Western name for the Kurdish Muslim ruler Salah al-Din ibn Ayyub: he lived from 1138 to 1193 AD, and was the renowned general who confronted the Crusaders in the Near East. Saladin and Richard the Lionheart, king of England, are two names that tend to dominate the Crusades. Both have gone down in Medieval history as great military leaders, though their impact was limited to the Third Crusade.[4] Eventually, these two—who respected each other greatly, according to legend—signed the Treaty of Ramla, which kept Jerusalem in Muslim hands, but opened the city for Christian pilgrimages.)

After the 1948 war, Jericho was controlled by Jordan. Many Arabs who left other parts of Palestine moved to the area and a number of UN refugee camps were set up. It's important to note that the city is still under Arab control today. While it's not uncommon to go through security checks in and out of Jericho, there's no need to worry or be afraid, for this town thrives on tourism and welcomes visitors.[5]

## JERICHO IN THE BIBLE

Jericho is one of the most famous places of the Bible. Although Moses was not allowed to enter, he stood on top of Mount Nebo to the east—directly across from Jericho—and saw the Promised Land:

*Then Moses climbed Mount Nebo from the plains of Moab to the top of Pisgah, across from Jericho. There the LORD showed him the whole land—from Gilead to Dan, all of Naphtali, the territory of Ephraim and Manasseh, all the land of Judah as far as the western sea, the Negev and the whole region from the Valley of Jericho, the City of Palms, as far as Zoar. Then the LORD said to him, "This is the land I promised on oath to Abraham, Isaac and Jacob when I said, 'I will give it to your descendants.' I have let you see it with your eyes, but you will not cross over into it." And Moses the servant of the LORD died there in Moab, as the LORD had said.* Deuteronomy 34:1-5

Jericho was also the hometown of Rahab, the harlot (Joshua 2:1). Rahab is later listed in the genealogies of both King David of Israel and of Jesus (Matthew 1:5). The Hebrew writer explains further:

*By faith the walls of Jericho fell, after the army had marched around them for seven days. By faith the prostitute Rahab, because she welcomed the spies, was not killed with those who were disobedient.* Hebrews 11:30-31

Many of us know the story of the fall of Jericho—how God directed the Israelites to circle the city once a day for six days. On the seventh day they were to circle the wall seven times. The people were to be led by seven priests walking beside the Ark of the Covenant and blowing rams' horns (shofarot). The priests blew their horns, the soldiers shouted, and the walls of the city fell (Joshua 6). What you may not remember is that once the city fell, Joshua placed this curse on Jericho:

*At that time Joshua pronounced this solemn oath: "Cursed before the LORD is the man who undertakes to rebuild this city, Jericho: "At the cost of his firstborn son will he lay its foundations; at the cost of his youngest will he set up its gates."* Joshua 6:26

His words would turn out to be prophetic. Centuries later, in the time of Ahab and Jezebel, Jericho was rebuilt:

*In Ahab's time, Hiel of Bethel rebuilt Jericho. He laid its foundations at the cost of his firstborn son Abiram, and he set up its gates at the cost of his youngest son Segub, in accordance with the word of the LORD spoken by Joshua son of Nun.* 1 Kings 16:34

By the time of the coming of Jesus Christ, Jericho was a busy city once again. John the Baptist baptized not far from Jericho and Jesus taught and healed in Jericho:

*Then they came to Jericho. As Jesus and his disciples, together with a large crowd, were leaving the city, a blind man, Bartimaeus (that is, the Son of Timaeus), was sitting by the roadside begging. When he heard that it was Jesus of Nazareth, he began to shout, "Jesus, Son of David, have mercy on me!" Many rebuked him and told him to be quiet, but he shouted all the more, "Son of David, have mercy on me!" Jesus stopped and said, "Call him." So they called to the blind man, "Cheer up! On your feet! He's calling you." Throwing his cloak aside, he jumped to his feet and came to Jesus. "What do you want me to do for you?" Jesus asked him. The blind man said, "Rabbi, I want to see." "Go," said Jesus, "your faith has healed you." Immediately he received his sight and followed Jesus along the road.* Mark 10:46-52

**Fact Finder**: *What is the name of the first place that the Israelites camped after crossing the Jordan into the Promised Land? Joshua 4:19*

The bus ride into Jericho is long, so it's a good time to catch up on reading this book, talk to a friend sitting near you, or take a little nap—or all three. There is deli-cious food in Jericho at a two-story restaurant near the excavation site, so you can enjoy a nice lunch. You can even have your photo taken with a camel afterward! Addition-ally, there are a few popular spots to buy pottery and glassware.

*Photo: Dudley Rutherford*

As you are arriving in Jericho, imagine what it was like 2,000 years ago when Jesus was enter-ing the city. The Lord's reputation had spread throughout Jericho, as evidenced by this ex-change with a man in the crowd who had struggled to just catch a glimpse of Jesus:

*Jesus entered Jericho and was passing through. A man was there by the name of Zacchaeus; he was a chief tax collector and was wealthy. He wanted to see who Jesus was, but being a short man he could not, be-cause of the crowd. So he ran ahead and climbed a sycamore-fig tree to see him, since Jesus was coming that way. When Jesus reached the spot, he looked up and said to him, "Zacchaeus, come down immediately. I must stay at your house today." So he came down at once and welcomed him gladly. All the people saw this and began to mutter, "He has gone to be the guest of a 'sinner.'" But Zacchaeus stood up and said to the Lord, "Look, Lord! Here and now I give half of my possessions to the poor, and if I have cheated anybody out of anything, I will pay back four times the amount." Jesus said to him, "Today salvation has come to this house, because this man, too, is a son of Abraham. For the Son of Man came to seek and to save what was lost." Luke 19:1-10*

After reading this story from Luke 19, I am always drawn to note that Jesus knows our name just as He knew Zacchaeus' name, and He desires to stay at our house as well. Are you looking for Jesus? Have you invited Him into your life and heart? Jesus desires to give you salvation if only you will open your heart and answer his invitation.

---

## JERUSALEM INTRODUCED

*Pray for the peace of Jerusalem: "May those who love you be secure. May there be peace within your walls and security within your citadels." For the sake of my brothers and friends, I will say, "Peace be within you." For the sake of the house of the LORD our God, I will seek your prosperity.*
Psalm 122:6-9

Jerusalem is a gorgeous dichotomy of old and new, east and west. Ancient buildings brimming with history and character are juxtaposed with tall, über modern edifices. You might see an orthodox Jewish man wearing a kippah (yarmulke) and clothing typical of the 18th century mid-European shtetls, or a heavily veiled woman carrying home groceries in plastic pails balanced on her head on the same street as young Israeli students in uniform, men and women in svelte business attire, and tourists or more progressive Jews in contemporary fashions. You will pass by new shops offering cellular phones and other state-of-the-art amenities, and moments later, you may find yourself wandering down a seeming alleyway filled with vendors selling spices, scarves, ceramics, beads, trinkets, and other colorful wares.

The sights, sounds, and smells of this city are manifold. Every stone here tells a wondrous story of a city that has drawn millions of faithful pilgrims for thousands of years. Jerusalem, the capital of Israel, offers excitement, adventure, and fascinating historic and archeological sites. There are also amazingly modern tourist attractions for all lovers of food, culture, the arts, theater, music, and architecture.[6]

An ordinance requires buildings to be constructed of the honey-colored limestone that is quarried nearby. When the sun rises and sets on the city, Jerusalem is positively luminous, much like fine gold. It's no wonder it has been called "Jerusalem the golden!"

The Holy City promises a religious and spiritual experience unlike any other place on earth (from the *Pilgrim's Progress*):

> This is the home of faith. Abraham Heschel said, "In order to see Jerusalem, you must hear it." At the Western Wall the pilgrim can hear above the quiet swaying chant of the Kedushah, the high-pitched call of the muezzin, bidding Muslims to prayer, and, in the background, the boom of bells from the Church of the Holy Sepulchre. This seems sometimes competitive, sometimes harmonious.

Contrasting sights within one city – Jerusalem                    *Photos: Dudley Rutherford*

The saga of God touching human life comes alive in this place for those who come as witnesses, not just onlookers, as pilgrims, not just tourists. To walk into Jerusalem is to walk into a dream, into a prayer. Teddy Kolleck, well-known former mayor, used to tell visitors, "From here a phone call 'upstairs' is not long distance."[7]

Jerusalem's Christian quarter alone houses some 40 religious buildings, such as churches, monasteries, and pilgrims' hostels. We will learn more about the specific sites in Jerusalem like the Old City, Four Quarters, Western Wall, and the Via Dolorosa in Chapters 8 and 10.

As mentioned in Chapter 1, Jerusalem's history is one of wars and struggles. Its strategic location near the Mediterranean Sea and trade routes attracted many nations that wanted to capture the city, and some of them did rule over it for various periods. This city has known war and peace, love and hate, riches and poverty, destruction and renewal, happiness and pain. But from the very beginning, Jerusalem has been the one and only—a unique city second to none in the entire world.

## JERUSALEM IN THE BIBLE

The fact that the name "Jerusalem" appears 801 times in the New International Version of the Bible makes it quite evident that this city is very important to and cherished by God and His people. An entire book could be written on Jerusalem and its biblical and historical significance, but we will simply highlight a few of the most notable places that Jerusalem is mentioned in the Word of God.

First, it was King David's choice for the capital city, "set on a commanding height of land that sprawls across a spine of limestone hills… Jerusalem is powerfully located for defense, for trade, and for beauty. The ancients referred to Jerusalem as the 'navel of the world,'"[8] because of the belief that it's where humanity actually began.

Second, many of the most familiar Psalms were actually written for Jewish pilgrims who were journeying to the Holy City. They would have come up to Jerusalem from lower ground singing, as was the accepted custom. Of special mention is Psalm 87. Note that the word "Zion" often refers to Jerusalem:

> *He has founded his city on the holy mountain.*
> *The LORD loves the gates of Zion*
> *more than all the other dwellings of Jacob.*
>
> *Glorious things are said of you,*
> *city of God:*
> *"I will record Rahab and Babylon*
> *among those who acknowledge me—*
> *Philistia too, and Tyre, along with Cush—*
> *and will say, 'This one was born in Zion.'"*
> *Indeed, of Zion it will be said,*
> *"This one and that one were born in her,*
> *and the Most High himself will establish her."*

*The LORD will write in the register of the peoples:*
*"This one was born in Zion."*

*As they make music they will sing,*
*"All my fountains are in you."*

The books of Isaiah, Jeremiah, Ezekiel, Daniel, and many others in the Old Testament contain numerous prophesies about the city of Jerusalem. When we get to the New Testament, we see that Paul visited Jerusalem multiple times, as mentioned in the books of Acts and Galatians.

But perhaps the most important mention of Jerusalem in the Bible concerns Jesus Christ, the Messiah and Son of the Living God. First, in Matthew 21:12-15, Jesus drives the moneychangers from God's house in Jerusalem and heals many:

*Jesus entered the temple courts and drove out all who were buying and sell-ing there. He overturned the tables of the moneychangers and the benches of those selling doves. "It is written," he said to them, "'My house will be called a house of prayer,' but you are making it 'a den of robbers.'" The blind and the lame came to him at the temple, and he healed them. But when the chief priests and the teachers of the law saw the wonderful things he did and the children shouting in the temple courts, "Hosanna to the Son of David," they were indignant.*

Next, in Matthew 23:37-39, He mourns for the Holy City, saying:

*"Jerusalem, Jerusalem, you who kill the prophets and stone those sent to you, how often I have longed to gather your children together, as a hen gathers her chicks under her wings, and you were not willing. Look, your house is left to you desolate. For I tell you, you will not see me again until you say, 'Blessed is he who comes in the name of the Lord.'"*

Finally, in John 12:12-19, He comes to Jerusalem as King, receiving the praises of the people and greatly upsetting the religious leaders:

*The next day the great crowd that had come for the festival heard that Je-sus was on his way to Jerusalem. They took palm branches and went out to meet him, shouting, "Hosanna!" "Blessed is he who comes in the name of the Lord!" "Blessed is the king of Israel!" Jesus found a young donkey and sat on it, as it is written: "Do not be afraid, Daughter Zion; see, your king is coming seated on a donkey's colt." At first his disciples did not understand all this.*

*Only after Jesus was glorified did they realize that these things had been written about him and that these things had been done to him. Now the crowd that was with him when he called Lazarus from the tomb and raised him from the dead continued to spread the word. Many people, because they had heard that he had performed this sign, went out to meet him. So the Pharisees said to one another, "See, this is getting us nowhere. Look how the whole world has gone after him!"*

Next, in Luke 19:41-44, Jesus mourns over the city and gives this startling prophecy:

*As he approached Jerusalem and saw the city, he wept over it and said, "If you, even you, had only known on this day what would bring you peace— but now it is hidden from your eyes. The days will come upon you when your enemies will build an embankment against you and encircle you and hem you in on every side. They will dash you to the ground, you and the children within your walls. They will not leave one stone on another, because you did not recognize the time of God's coming to you."*

Finally, the book of Revelation speaks of the ultimate glory of Jerusalem. Take a look at this stunning description:

*Then I saw "a new heaven and a new earth," for the first heaven and the first earth had passed away, and there was no longer any sea. I saw the Holy City, the new Jerusalem, coming down out of heaven from God, prepared as a bride beautifully dressed for her husband. And I heard a loud voice from the throne saying, "Look! God's dwelling place is now among the people, and he will dwell with them. They will be his people, and God himself will be with them and be their God. 'He will wipe every tear from their eyes. There will be no more death' or mourning or crying or pain, for the old order of things has passed away." He who was seated on the throne said, "I am making everything new!" Then he said, "Write this down, for these words are trustworthy and true." He said to me: "It is done. I am the Alpha and the Omega, the Beginning and the End. To the thirsty I will give water without cost from the spring of the water of life. Those who are victorious will inherit all this, and I will be their God and they will be my children. But the cowardly, the unbelieving, the vile, the murderers, the sexually immoral, those who practice magic arts, the idolaters and all liars—they will be consigned to the fiery lake of burning sulfur. This is the second death." One of the seven angels who had the seven bowls full of the seven last plagues came and said to me, "Come,*

*I will show you the bride, the wife of the Lamb." And he carried me away in the Spirit to a mountain great and high, and showed me the Holy City, Jerusalem, coming down out of heaven from God. It shone with the glory of God, and its brilliance was like that of a very precious jewel, like a jasper, clear as crystal. It had a great, high wall with twelve gates, and with twelve angels at the gates. On the gates were written the names of the twelve tribes of Israel. There were three gates on the east, three on the north, three on the south and three on the west. The wall of the city had twelve foundations, and on them were the names of the twelve apostles of the Lamb.* Revelation 21:1-14

When seeing Jerusalem for the very first time, a flood of emotions surge throughout one's soul. This is the ancient City of David, the City of Zion, the spiritual capital of both Jews and Christians. Upon entering this city, your life will never be the same. Beyond brick and mortar, there is a spiritual dimension that will bring you into the presence of God.

Tomorrow we will begin visiting some of the many sites that have been preserved for the past 2,000 years. Take a moment to thank the Lord for His mercy and kindness to you for enabling you to make this journey.

Note: One of my favorite things to do after checking into the hotel and having dinner is to catch a cab and visit the Western Wall at night. We will discuss the importance of the Wall in Chapter 8, but if you're not too tired, join with a few friends for safety purposes, hail a cab, and visit the Western Wall after the sun goes down. It will be well-lit and open all night with people praying. The experience is quite surreal; you feel as if you're on a Hollywood movie set, but in reality you will be standing at one of the holiest sites in all of Jerusalem. Be respectful to those who are praying, bring a humble heart—and a handkerchief to wipe your tears—and be ready to be moved beyond your imagination. You won't want to leave, but you must, for tomorrow you will embark an adventure that is sure to knock your sandals off. Enjoy, be blessed, and welcome to Jerusalem!

*Top:* Welcome to the old city of Jerusalem.

*Above:* Visitors are encouraged to walk to the top of the hill in the background to take in the view of Beth She'an.

*Above right:* Hot air was pushed through stone pillars supporting marble floors in this Beth She'an bath house.

*Right:* Columns still standing at Beth She'an remind us of the incredible history that has taken place on this site since even before King Saul's time.

*Photos: Steve Beaumont*

# JOURNAL: JORDAN RIVER VALLEY

# JOURNAL: JORDAN RIVER VALLEY

_____

_____

_____

_____

_____

_____

_____

_____

_____

_____

_____

_____

_____

_____

_____

_____

_____

_____

_____

_____

_____

_____

_____

_____

_____

**Fact Finder**: _In Jesus' famous parable of "the good Samaritan," the man whom the Samaritan helped was on a journey from Jerusalem to what city?_ Luke 10:30-34

# JOURNAL: JORDAN RIVER VALLEY

MODEL CITY
MOUNT OF OLIVES
GARDEN OF GETHSEMANE
EAST GATE
KIDRON VALLEY
ABSALOM'S TOMB

# CHAPTER 7: MOUNT OF OLIVES

## MODEL CITY

*He told them, "This is what is written: The Messiah will suffer and rise from the dead on the third day, and repentance for the forgiveness of sins will be preached in his name to all nations, beginning at Jerusalem. You are witnesses of these things."* Luke 24:46-48

To get a good idea of what Jerusalem looked like in Jesus' day (the period of the Second Temple, 516 BC-70 AD), visit the complete model of the ancient city, which is located at the Israel Museum in Jerusalem.

Model City in Jerusalem                                    Photo: Melissa Robles

If possible, go early in the day to get your bearings. The model is 1/50th the size of Jerusalem, but the attention to detail is amazing. The same materials that were used in the actual city are used here including stone, wood, copper, and iron.

Hans Kroch, a Jewish banker, had the model built to honor his son who fell in the Israeli War of Independence. Professor Michael Avi-

Yonah of the Hebrew University was put in charge of the project. Using the writings of Josephus Flavius (a 1st century historian), the New Testament, Jewish sources, and his knowledge of the architecture of the time period, he constructed the model.

Try to imagine the sun setting over this city. Flavius described the Temple "like a snowy mountain glittering in the sun." Look at the height of the walls—just 28 inches high in the model but 115 feet high in real life. That's taller than a 10-story building! The vulnerable north side of Jerusalem was defended by three of these walls like stone waves rippling away from the city. Deep valleys surrounded the city on the west, south, and east sides; so these walls protected the only vulnerable side.

Pay attention to the three towers built by King Herod to protect his palace. The largest, 150 feet high, was called Phasael, after Herod's brother; the second, Hippicus, 130 feet high, was named after an unknown friend of the king; and the third, 90 feet high, was called Mariamne after Herod's queen, whom he condemned to death. Her tower is more ornate than the other two towers, because, in the words of Josephus, "the king considered it appropriate that the tower, named after a woman, should surpass in decoration those called after men."

The model is constantly being updated as archeological finds provide new information. For example, you can now see a replica of luxurious private buildings that were just recently uncovered in the Jewish Quarter. The buildings included large rooms decorated with frescoes and mosaics, bathrooms, water cisterns, and ritual baths.

Here is a list of other things you must do when you're at the Model City:

- Locate Antonia Fortress.
- Locate Solomon's Porch (where there were 162 Corinthian columns).
- Find the Jerusalem Theater.
- Make sure someone points out to you the Pools of Bethesda, because you will see them shortly.
- And of course, the crown jewel is to see the Second Temple, which is Herod's Temple—the same Temple that Jesus would have walked into—and it is viewed as Jesus would have seen it.

On your own, see if you can find the section of the wall that is now known as the "Western Wall." If you can't locate it, be sure to ask your guide to point it out for you.

Standing over this model of Jerusalem gives you a sort of God's eye view. Use it to orient yourself, get the big picture, and then go visit the actual excavation sites. To view the Model City online, visit the following interactive site that provides a fascinating virtual tour: www. imj.org.il/panavision/model_pre_3eng.html. We will elaborate more on the rest of the interesting things located at the Israel Museum in Chapter 10.[1]

## Mount of Olives

*While they were eating, Jesus took bread, gave thanks and broke it, and gave it to his disciples, saying, "Take and eat; this is my body." Then he took the cup, gave thanks and offered it to them, saying, "Drink from it, all of you. This is my blood of the covenant, which is poured out for many for the forgiveness of sins. I tell you, I will not drink of this fruit of the vine from now on until that day when I drink it anew with you in my Father's kingdom." When they had sung a hymn, they went out to the Mount of Olives.* Matthew 26:26-30

The Mount of Olives is a limestone ridge located just a few hundred yards east of the Temple Mount in Jerusalem. It offers a breathtakingly beautiful view of the Old City, rising more than 2,000 feet above the Kidron Valley, which separates Jerusalem from the Mount of Olives. Some tour guides elect to spend some time atop this ridge and give a brief synopsis of Jerusalem's history. It is truly a priceless experience to get this fascinating history lesson while looking across the valley, seeing so many old and new buildings and the golden Dome of the Rock, and imagining what life would have been like in Jesus' day.

The Mount of Olives, named for its ancient olive groves, is home to an estimated 150,000 graves, including tombs from biblical times traditionally associated with Zechariah and Absalom. Important rabbis from the 15th to the 20th centuries are buried here, as well as former Israeli prime minister Menachem Begin. The site is a mountainside of stones. You see, Jews traditionally do not bring flowers to a grave; instead they leave a small stone on the grave, symbolically raising a monument for the loved one.

You may notice that the cemetery is in pretty bad condition, and you may wonder why such a holy site is in such bad shape. Well, during the 19-year Jordanian occupation, 40,000 to 50,000 tombs were desecrated and much of the cemetery was vandalized. The Jordanians even cut a road right through the heart of the cemetery, which destroyed thousands of graves—some dating back to the time of the First Temple.

But despite so much death and destruction both past and present, there is hope. Jewish tradition says that the Messiah will come from the east, pass the Mount of Olives and continue through the Kidron Valley before arriving at the Temple Mount. They believe the dead will rise on that day and escort Him into the city. Jews from around the world often ask to be buried near Jerusalem, for they believe they will be among the first to greet the Messiah. Landmarks on the Mount of Olives include Yad Avshalom, the Tomb of Zechariah, Gethsemane, Bethphage, and Mary's Tomb.

There are also many churches atop the Mount of Olives, such as:
• The Church of All Nations (Basilica of the Agony).
• The Church of Mary Magdalene.
• Dominus Flevit (The Lord Wept).
• The Evangelical Sisterhood of Mary.
• Little Family of the Resurrection.
• Pater Noster (Church of the Lord's Prayer).
• Augusta Victoria Lutheran Hospital, Church & Tower.
• The Russian Orthodox Convent of the Ascension & Bell Tower.

Also found on the Mount of Olives is the Chapel of the Ascension. This chapel was built in 392 AD to mark the site where Jesus ascended into heaven. The original chapel was destroyed by the Persians and rebuilt by the Crusaders. The current chapel was built on the ruins of that 7th century church. After the Crusaders were driven out by Saladin, the chapel was converted to a mosque.

## Mount of Olives in the Bible

This hill was first referred to in the Bible in 2 Samuel 15:30, when King David fled the city to escape from Absalom's rebellion. Next, King Solomon erected altars dedicated to false, foreign gods here on the mount (1 Kings 11:7). They were later destroyed by King Josiah who "filled it with bones" to prevent future worship, and by this it had become known as the Hill of Corruption (2 Kings 23:13-14).

*Top left:* Dominus Flevit view of Jerusalem. *Top right:* Russian Orthodox Church of Mary Magdalene. *Bottom left:* Church of All Nations. *Bottom right:* Inside the Chapel of Ascension which is built over the site where Jesus may have ascended to heaven. *Photos: Todd Bolen*

When Ezekiel had the vision of the cherubim and the wheels, the glory of the Lord went up from the city and hovered above this mountain (Ezekiel 11:22-23). Additionally, the people gathered olive branches here for the first Feast of Tabernacles after their return from the Babylonian exile (Nehemiah 8:15).

It's hard to grasp how central this place was in the life of Jesus. Let's just review some of the big events that happened here. Jesus stood on the Mount of Olives and prophesied Jerusalem's destruction:

*"The days will come upon you when your enemies will build an embankment against you and encircle you and hem you in on every side. They will dash you to the ground, you and the children within your walls. They will not leave one stone on another, because you did not recognize the time of God's coming to you."* Luke 19:43-44

In 70 AD, the Roman commander Titus stood on this very hill and oversaw Jerusalem's destruction, unknowingly fulfilling Jesus' words. The Mount of Olives played a strategic role as Titus positioned his headquarters on the northern extension of the ridge during the siege of Jerusalem. He named the place Mount Scopus, or "Lookout Hill," because of the view it offered over the city walls. The whole hill must have provided a platform for the Roman catapults that hurled heavy objects over the Jewish fortifications of the city. Take a moment to pray for the peace of Israel.

Jesus taught here. He often traveled over the mount on His way to Bethany to visit His friend Lazarus. His triumphal entry into Jerusalem on a donkey took place over and down the Mount of Olives (Luke 19:28-44). He prayed with His disciples here just before His arrest (Luke 22:39-54). Here, the Lord was betrayed by Judas' kiss and then performed one of His last miracles by restoring the soldier's ear that Peter had sliced off. Jesus appeared to the disciples on the Mount of Olives after His resurrection, and He ascended into heaven from here (Acts 1:1-12). Here are some other biblical passages concerning this amazing site:

*Then the Lord will go out and fight against those nations, as he fights in the day of battle. On that day his feet will stand on the Mount of Olives, east of Jerusalem, and the Mount of Olives will be split in two from east to west, forming a great valley, with half of the mountain moving north and half moving south. You will flee by my mountain valley, for it will extend to Azel. You will flee as you fled from the earthquake in the days of Uzziah king of Judah. Then the Lord my God will come, and all the holy ones with Him.* Zechariah 14:3-5

*"At that time the sign of the Son of Man will appear in the sky, and all the nations of the earth will mourn. They will see the Son of Man coming on the clouds of the sky, with power and great glory. And he will send his angels with a loud trumpet call, and they will gather his elect from the four winds, from one end of the heavens to the other."* Matthew 24:30-31

*After he said this, he was taken up before their very eyes, and a cloud hid him from their sight. They were looking intently up into the sky as he was going, when suddenly two men dressed in white stood beside them. "Men of Galilee," they said, "why do you stand here looking into the sky? This same*

*Jesus, who has been taken from you into heaven, will come back in the same way you have seen him go into heaven."* Acts 1:9-11[2]

**Fact Finder**: *During the Olivet prophecy, Jesus warned us that prior to His return there would be how many false "Christs" and false prophets in the world?*
Matthew 24:4-5, 23-25

From atop the Mount of Olives, Jesus looked across the valley towards Jerusalem from the same vantage point you have today, except for one difference: Jesus wept.

*As He approached Jerusalem and saw the city, he wept over it and said, "If you, even you, had only known on this day what would bring you peace—but now it is hidden from your eyes."* Luke 19:41-42

Imagine His broken heart and his emotion for the nation that rejected the one Person who could save them—the One who could bring them peace. In a matter of days, Jesus would go to the cross and die for the sins of the world, yet Israel did not recognize Him as the Messiah. Don't you see that not much has changed in the last 2,000 years, in that Jerusalem and Israel as a whole still reject Jesus as Messiah and the fulfillment of all the Old Testament prophesies?

Like Jesus, our hearts should break and our tears should flow as we look across the landscape and see the city of Jerusalem and the peace that eludes her. May we pray for people of Israel—that they would recognize that Jesus is indeed the King of kings and the Lord of lords, and that they would understand He is Messiah, the Christ, the Son of the Living God. Why not write out your prayer for Jerusalem in the space below?

_____

_____

_____

_____

_____

_____

## GARDEN OF GETHSEMANE

*When he had finished praying, Jesus left with his disciples and crossed the Kidron Valley. On the other side there was a garden, and he and his disciples went into it.* John 18:1

Within the Garden of Gethsemane is the Basilica of the Agony also known as the Church of All Nations. Built in 1924 on the traditional site of the Garden of Gethsemane, the Basilica of the Agony enshrines a section of bedrock identified as the place where Jesus prayed alone in the garden on the night of His arrest. There is even a grove of ancient olive trees here. Olive trees don't have rings, so their age can't be precisely determined, but scholars estimate the age of these trees to be anywhere between one and two thousand years old.

Olive trees in the Garden of Gethsemane       Jerusalem's Golden Gate (East gate)
Photo: Steve Beaumont                          Photo: Dudley Rutherford

Although it is not certain that this is the exact spot, the setting does fit the Gospel description, and the present church rests on the foundation of two earlier shrines—a 12th century Crusader chapel, abandoned in 1345, and a 4th century Byzantine basilica, destroyed by an earthquake in 746.

The Church of All Nations is plain by European standards, though it has beautiful murals depicting the events that took place in Gethsemane. Notice the colorful mosaic over the entrance, which represents the acceptance of Jesus by the world. The windows in the church dimly light the interior, and a sculpture of thorns in the middle of the church represents the spot where Jesus prayed. Notice the mosaic tiles inside each of the 12 cupolas depicting the national emblems of donor communities. These emblems are what gave this church its nickname, the Church of All Nations. From the front of the Basilica looking westward, you can see the Golden Gate, one of the gates of Jerusalem.

After Jesus' arrest He was taken a short distance up the hill to where Dominus Flevit Church now stands. Dominus Flevit, which means "the Lord wept," is a tear-drop shaped building. The church marks where Jesus stood and wept over Jerusalem's coming destruction.

## Garden of Gethsemane in the Bible

After eating the Last Supper with His disciples, and before His betrayal and arrest, Jesus spent the night in the Garden of Gethsemane. Take a moment to think about what Jesus went through that night, asking if this cup could be passed from Him, but ultimately yielding His will to God the Father's. The name of this garden, Gethsemane, means "olive press." Just as the olives here were pressed, crushing the oil out of them, He too would soon be pressed "pouring Himself out even unto death" (Isaiah 53:12).

*While they were eating, Jesus took bread, and when he had given thanks, he broke it and gave it to his disciples, saying, "Take and eat; this is my body."*

*Then he took a cup, and when he had given thanks, he gave it to them, saying, "Drink from it, all of you. This is my blood of the covenant, which is poured out for many for the forgiveness of sins. I tell you, I will not drink from this fruit of the vine from now on until that day when I drink it new with you in my Father's kingdom."*

*When they had sung a hymn, they went out to the Mount of Olives.*

*Then Jesus told them, "This very night you will all fall away on account of me, for it is written: "'I will strike the shepherd, and the sheep of the flock will be scattered.' But after I have risen, I will go ahead of you into Galilee."*

*Peter replied, "Even if all fall away on account of you, I never will."*

*"Truly I tell you," Jesus answered, "this very night, before the rooster crows, you will disown me three times."*

*But Peter declared, "Even if I have to die with you, I will never disown you." And all the other disciples said the same.*

*Then Jesus went with his disciples to a place called Gethsemane, and he said to them, "Sit here while I go over there and pray." He took Peter and the two sons of Zebedee along with him, and he began to be sorrowful and troubled. Then he said to them, "My soul is overwhelmed with sorrow to the point of death. Stay here and keep watch with me."*

*Going a little farther, he fell with his face to the ground and prayed, "My Father, if it is possible, may this cup be taken from me. Yet not as I will, but as you will."*

*Then he returned to his disciples and found them sleeping. "Couldn't you men keep watch with me for one hour?" he asked Peter. "Watch and pray so that you will not fall into temptation. The spirit is willing, but the flesh is weak."*

*He went away a second time and prayed, "My Father, if it is not possible for this cup to be taken away unless I drink it, may your will be done."*

*When he came back, he again found them sleeping, because their eyes were heavy. So he left them and went away once more and prayed the third time, saying the same thing.*

*Then he returned to the disciples and said to them, "Are you still sleeping and resting? Look, the hour has come, and the Son of Man is delivered into the hands of sinners. Rise! Let us go! Here comes my betrayer!"*

*While he was still speaking, Judas, one of the Twelve, arrived. With him was a large crowd armed with swords and clubs, sent from the chief priests and the elders of the people. Now the betrayer had arranged a signal with them: "The one I kiss is the man; arrest him." Going at once to Jesus, Judas said, "Greetings, Rabbi!" and kissed him.*

*Jesus replied, "Do what you came for, friend."*

*Then the men stepped forward, seized Jesus and arrested him.*
Matthew 26:26-50

## The East Gate (Golden Gate)

*The glory of the LORD entered the temple through the gate facing east.*
Ezekiel 43:4

From the Mount of Olives, look toward the west at the wall around Old City Jerusalem and you will see a large, double gate that looks permanently locked. The East Gate (or Golden Gate) is the oldest of the current gates in Jerusalem's Old City Walls. According to Jewish tradition, the Shekhinah (Divine Presence) used to appear through this gate, and will appear again when the Messiah comes (Ezekiel 44:1-3) and a new gate will replace the present one.

In ancient times, Jews used to pray for mercy at the old East Gate—hence the name Sha'ar Harachamim (the Gate of Mercy). It was also known as the Beautiful Gate. In Christian apocryphal texts, the gate was the scene of a meeting between the parents of Mary. In Arabic, it is known as the Gate of Eternal Life. The Muslims call this gate The Mercy Gate (Bab el Rahmeh) and according to the Koran, the just will pass through this gate on the Day of Judgment.

Remains of a much older gate dating to the times of the Second Jewish Temple have been found here. The present gate was probably built around 520 AD as part of Justinian I's building program in Jerusalem. During the time of the First Temple, the East Gate was the main entrance into the Temple area.

If you stand on the Mount of Olives, you can look over the East Gate into the huge area north of the Dome of the Rock and see the East Gate, the Outer Court Gate, the Inner Court Gate, and the Temple entrance all in a perfect line. The Talmud makes this observation: "All the walls which were there were high, except the wall in the east, so that the priest who burned the heifer, standing on the top of the Mount of Olives, and directing himself to look, saw through the gateway of the sanctuary, at the time when he sprinkled the blood" (Mishnah, Middot 2:4). The Shekhinah, which used to appear through this gate, will appear again; but until then, the gate must be left untouched.

## The East Gate in the Bible

Four of Jerusalem's 11 gates are sealed, and the East Gate is one of them. Knowing that the Jews expected the Messiah to come through this gate, the Arabs decided to try to prevent any possibility of His return. Therefore, the East Gate was walled up by Muslim conquerors (the Ottoman Turks) with great stones in 1530 AD. A cemetery was planted in front of it because they thought that the Jewish Messiah could not set foot in a cemetery and therefore would not be able to come. Ironically, in sealing up the gate, they were actually fulfilling a prophecy made by Ezekiel (see below) about 600 years before Christ, which said that the gate would be shut. Think about that—God used even His enemies to fulfill His prophecy!

*Then the man brought me back to the outer gate of the sanctuary, the one facing east, and it was shut. The LORD said to me, "This gate is to remain shut. It must not be opened; no one may enter through it. It is to remain shut because the LORD, the God of Israel, has entered through it. The prince himself is the only one who may sit inside the gateway to eat in the presence of the LORD. He is to enter by way of the portico of the gateway and go out the same way."* Ezekiel 44:1-3

As Jesus entered Jerusalem through the East Gate, the people laid down palms and cried "Hosanna!" (John 12:13). This happened around 30 AD, long before the gate was blocked by the Ottomans. Our Lord rode on a donkey through the original East Gate, which was later destroyed along with the rest of the city by the Romans in 70 AD. Ezekiel says concerning this closed gate that the "Prince" (a word used in the Old Testament to refer to the coming Messiah and in the New Testament to refer to Jesus) shall enter it again. Jesus, having entered the city, said He would not be seen again until Jerusalem acknowledges Him (Matthew 23:37-39).[3]

---

Today the Temple Mount is under Muslim control, and the East (Golden) Gate is guarded around-the-clock, sealed up, and blocked off. The faulty thinking would be funny if it weren't so tragic. Arabs try to shut Jesus out with a wall just as the Romans tried to shut Him in with a stone. They put a cemetery at the gate not grasping the fact that this Messiah has no trouble walking through cemeteries—after all, He walked out of His own tomb. One day, the Messiah will arrive at the Mount of Olives with all His saints and He will once again depart from another cemetery and walk through another stone, the East Gate. Then the Lord will enter the Temple area.

The picture God is giving us here—in big blocks of stone—is this: Israel had access to God as His presence resided in the Holy of Holies (or, "the Most Holy Place," referred to in Exodus 26:33-34; Leviticus 16; 1 Kings 6:16 and more), but their hearts were so closed to Him that they did not recognize His Son. This gate stands as a monument to their closed hearts. For now the gate is shut, but that seal is as temporary as the one that was placed on His tomb. Jesus prophesied to Israel about the desolation of their Temple, and that desolation continues to this very day. But on the day of the His choosing, He will return, open the gate, re-build the Temple, and all Israel will know that the Lord is God.

---

## Kidron Valley

*When he had finished praying, Jesus left with his disciples and crossed the Kidron Valley. On the other side there was a garden, and he and his disciples went into it. Now Judas, who betrayed him, knew the place, because Jesus had often met there with his disciples. So Judas came to the garden, guiding a detachment of soldiers and some officials from the chief priests and the Pharisees. They were carrying torches, lanterns and weapons. Jesus, knowing all that was going to happen to him, went out and asked them, "Who is it you want?" "Jesus of Nazareth," they replied. "I am he," Jesus said. (And Judas the traitor was standing there with them.)* John 18:1-5

In the 1st century, the Kidron Valley was 50 feet lower than the valley floor you see today. That's about the height (or in this case, the depth) of a five-story building. Why the change in altitude? Rubble from the destroyed Temple and other rubbish was tossed down here.

Jerusalem was protected by the Kidron Valley to the east and the Hin-nom Valley to the west. These valleys merge south of the city from where the Wadi Kidron continues eastward to the Dead Sea. Viewed from the south, these two valleys look kind of like an off-center wish-bone, with the Kidron Valley on the right and the Hinnom Valley curving around in an "L" shape from the west. At one time a spring ran through the valley, but it was diverted by Hezekiah's tunnel to supply water to Jerusalem.

The Pool of Gihon is located in the Kidron Valley. The Kidron Brook runs through the valley during the wet season, but it remains dry most of the year.

Junction of Hinnom and Kidron Valleys     Absalom's Tomb          *Photos: Todd Bolen*

## Kidron Valley in the Bible

King David crossed the Kidron Valley to escape from his rebellious son Absalom (2 Samuel 15:23). King Asa burned his grandmother's pagan Asherah pole in the Kidron Valley (1 Kings 15:13), and the evil Athaliah was executed there (2 Kings 11:16). It became for some time a dumping site for destroyed pagan items (2 Chronicles 29:16, 30:14). By the time of King Josiah, the Kidron Valley had become the city cemetery (2 Kings 23:6; Jeremiah 26:23). For this reason, the valley has been of much interest to archaeologists.

Jesus would have traveled through the Kidron Valley many times as He traveled to and from Jerusalem.[4]

**Fact Finder:** *The whole valley where the dead bodies and ashes are thrown and all the terraces of the Kidron Valley will one day be called what to the Lord?* Jeremiah 31:38-40

## Absalom's Tomb

The traditional site of the tomb of David's rebellious son, Absalom, is located on the eastern slope of the Kidron Valley, on the east side of Jerusalem. Josephus wrote about this tomb, which existed in the 1st century AD. It stands 20 feet high and 24 feet wide.

In Judaism, rebellious children were taught to throw stones at "Yad Avshalom," the shrine of Absalom, to learn what rebellion leads to. "If anyone in Jerusalem has a disobedient child, he shall take him out to the Valley of Jehoshaphat, to Absalom's Monument, and force him, by words or stripes, to hurl stones at it, and to curse Absalom; meanwhile telling him the life and fate of that rebellious son."

Yikes! This seems a little harsh, right? But before we begin to feel too sorry for Absalom, let's review his life's highlight reel from 2 Samuel: 13-15:

• Absalom's sister Tamar is raped, rejected, and shamed by her half-brother Amnon.
• Tamar receives no justice from King David.
• Two years later, Absalom conspires and kills Amnon.
• Now a murderer, Absalom flees and remains banished.
• David, mourning Amnon and Absalom, calls for Absalom's return after three years.
• David, still divided in heart, remains distant for two more years without seeing Absalom.
• Absalom burns down General Joab's field to gain the King's attention.
• Absalom's tantrum gets David's attention and they are reconciled, somewhat.
• Absalom conspires to overthrow David.
• Absalom exploits the hurts of Israel's citizens.
• Absalom steals their allegiance.

*In the course of time, Absalom provided himself with a chariot and horses and with fifty men to run ahead of him. He would get up early and stand by the side of the road leading to the city gate. Whenever anyone came with a complaint to be placed before the king for a decision, Absalom would call out to him, "What town are you from?" He would answer, "Your servant is from one of the tribes of Israel." Then Absalom would say to him, "Look, your claims are valid and proper, but there is no representative of the king to hear you." And Absalom* Absalom's tomb    *Photo: Todd Bolen*

*would add, "If only I were appointed judge in the land! Then everyone who has a complaint or case could come to me and I would see that he gets justice." Also, whenever anyone approached him to bow down before him, Absalom would reach out his hand, take hold of him and kiss him. Absalom behaved in this way toward all the Israelites who came to the king asking for justice, and so he stole the hearts of the men of Israel.* 2 Samuel 15:1-6

Looking back, we know that the flawed hero is David, the villain is Absalom, and that God, though disciplining David for his own sins, kept His promises and restored David to his throne. Had we been alive in those days, would we have chosen to stand with David or sided with the great majority who supported the rebel Absalom?

Without a doubt, Absalom (more specifically, Tamar) had been terribly wronged, but Absalom's response to injustice is what separated this father and son. Remember, David knew all about injustice. Murderous Saul hunted David and chased him into the wilderness. David was forced to live like a fugitive for years, but when the Lord put Saul's very life into David's hands, he refused to take vengeance. Compare that to Absalom's response to injustice. He plotted and carried out his vengeance, refusing to leave it in the hands of the Lord.

Read 2 Samuel chapter 15-18 to see how this family drama played out. Ultimately, Absalom died a less-than-honorable death, alone on the back of his mule with his neck caught in the branches of an oak tree (2 Samuel 18:9). When King David heard the news, instead of rejoicing over the death of this disobedient and disrespectful son, he mourned his loss.

*The king was shaken. He went up to the room over the gateway and wept. As he went, he said: "O my son Absalom! My son, my son Absalom! If only I had died instead of you – O Absalom, my son, my son!"*
2 Samuel 18:33

---

*Opposite page:* Aerial view of Jerusalem looking toward the west          Photo: Todd Bolen

A. The "First Wall" dates to 167 BC. Behind this section are ruins of the City of David.
B. 150,000 graves and tombs including the Tomb of Absalom.
C. One remaining wall from Solomon's Temple – The Western Wall – is located here.
D. Old City of Jerusalem is about 1/3 square mile surrounded by city walls.
E. Dome of the Rock sits on the original Solomon's Temple Mount location.
F. The sealed East Gate also called The Golden Gate.
G. Area of the Mount of Olives and the Garden of Gethsemene.
H. The Kidron Valley lies between Jerusalem and Mount of Olives.

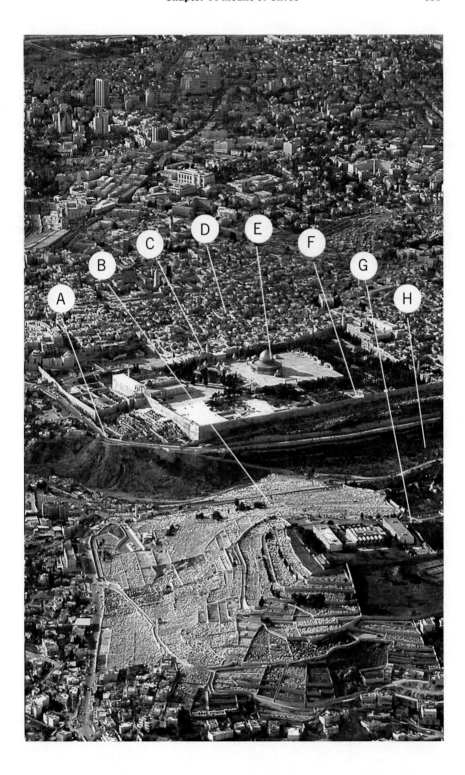

## JOURNAL: MOUNT OF OLIVES

# Journal: Mount of Olives

_____

_____

_____

_____

_____

_____

_____

_____

_____

_____

_____

_____

_____

_____

_____

_____

_____

_____

_____

_____

_____

_____

_____

_____

_____

_____

_____

_____

OLD CITY JERUSALEM
GATES OF THE OLD CITY
FOUR QUARTERS OF THE OLD CITY
WESTERN WALL
RABBI'S TUNNEL
HEZEKIAH'S TUNNEL
TEMPLE MOUNT

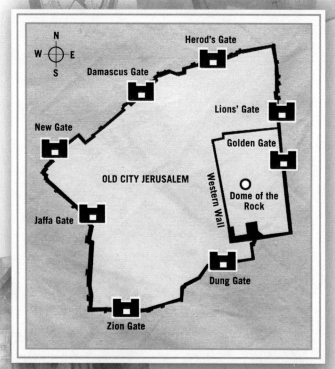

DOME OF THE ROCK
AL-AQSA MOSQUE
SAINT ANNE'S CHURCH
POOL OF BETHESDA
CHURCH OF THE
    HOLY SEPULCHRE
VIA DOLOROSA

# Chapter 8: Jerusalem

## Old City Jerusalem

*Pray for the peace of Jerusalem: "May those who love you be secure. May there be peace within your walls and security within your citadels." For the sake of my brothers and friends, I will say, "Peace be within you." For the sake of the house of the LORD our God, I will seek your prosperity.*
Psalm 122:6-9

It's fun to wander the narrow, centuries-old streets of the Old City          *Photos: Todd Bolen*

In the film, *Raiders of the Lost Ark*, Indiana Jones' archenemy pats the ark and says, "You and I are just passing through history. This is history." When you arrive in the Old City of Jerusalem, that is precisely the feeling you get. Just walking through the narrow streets and alleys—knowing that this is a holy place to three of the largest faiths in the world—gives you the sense that you have stepped back in time. And it's not just that you are studying history, for you are actually walking through it.

The Old City covers roughly 220 acres and the surrounding walls date back to Suleiman the Magnificent (1520-1566 AD). Traditionally, the Old City has been divided into four quarters, although the modern boundaries only date back to the 19th century. Today, the Old City is roughly divided into the Muslim Quarter, the Christian Quarter, the Jewish Quarter, and the Armenian Quarter. The Jewish Quarter of the Old City was largely destroyed by Jordan following the 1948 Arab-Israeli War, and was later restored by Israel following the 1967 Six-Day War.

Dome of the Rock                    Western Wall        *Photos: Dudley Rutherford*

The heart of the Old City is the Temple Mount, which is recognized by Jews, Christians, and Muslims as the site of Abraham's sacrifice. The Dome of the Rock, built in the 7th century and decorated with beautiful geometric and floral motifs, dominates this wide, open space. When the Romans destroyed the Second Temple in 70 AD, only one outer wall surrounding the Temple Mount remained standing: today's Western Wall (or Wailing Wall).

The Old City was originally built by King David in 1004 BC and has long been considered the center of the world. In fact, ancient maps show Europe, Asia, and Africa, in a circle with Jerusalem at their center. This was the place where the Jews built the Temple, where Jesus was crucified, and where it's said Muhammad rose to heaven. Pilgrims, beggars, merchants, students, scholars, warriors, and slaves have all walked these streets.

Surrounding the Old City is a limestone wall. The top is open to the public and from here you can get a bird's-eye view of the city. To get in or out of the Old City, you walk through one of its numerous gates. There are a total of 11 gates, but only seven are open: Jaffa, Zion, Dung,

Lions', Herod's, Damascus, and New.

Make sure to notice the sharp, 90-degree turn of the original gates. This was to prevent enemies on horseback from charging full-speed through them. It also prevented the use of a long battering ram. At Zion Gate, look up and notice the holes that were used to pour boiling liquids onto attackers.

Zion Gate          Jaffa Gate          *Photos: Todd Bolen*

The main entrance to the city is the Jaffa Gate, built by Suleiman in 1538 AD. The name in Arabic, Bab el-Halil, or Hebron Gate, means "The Beloved," and refers to Abraham, the beloved of God who is buried in Hebron. A road allows cars to enter the city here. It was built in 1898 so that the German emperor, Kaiser Wilhelm II, could enter Jerusalem without leaving his carriage. Contrast that to how the King of Kings entered Jerusalem:

*As they approached Jerusalem and came to Bethphage on the Mount of Olives, Jesus sent two disciples, saying to them, "Go to the village ahead of you, and at once you will find a donkey tied there, with her colt by her. Untie them and bring them to me. If anyone says anything to you, tell him that the Lord needs them, and he will send them right away." This took place to fulfill what was spoken through the prophet: "Say to the Daughter of Zion, 'See, your king comes to you, gentle and riding on a donkey, on a colt, the foal of a donkey.'" The disciples went and did as Jesus had instructed them. They brought the donkey and the colt, placed their cloaks on them, and Jesus sat on them. A very large crowd spread their cloaks on the road, while others cut branches from the trees and spread them on the road. The crowds that went ahead of him and those that followed shouted, "Hosanna to the Son of David!" "Blessed is he who comes in the name of the Lord!"*

*"Blessed is he who comes in the name of the Lord!" "Hosanna in the highest!" When Jesus entered Jerusalem, the whole city was stirred and asked, "Who is this?" The crowds answered, "This is Jesus, the prophet from Nazareth in Galilee."* Matthew 21:1-11

Once you enter this gate, every square inch of the Old City has a story to tell. Stay alert to the sights and sounds around you and try to grasp the fact that you are walking in the very city where Jesus walked, breathing the same air, and praying to the same Father. [1]

---

If you have some time, it's a must to do some shopping within the narrow streets of the Old City, and the Jaffa Gate is the best place to begin. (You will learn more about Jaffa Gate and the rest of Jerusalem's gates in the next section.) The shops in the Old City are filled with souvenirs, pottery, clothing, food, and spices. Take it all in—the sights, smells, and sounds—and thank the Lord once again for giving you an opportunity to visit His city.

POINTS FROM THE PASTOR

It's easy to get lost, so I suggest you bring along a good map. I would also warn you not to shop alone. It's relatively safe, but as a tour guide once told me, "Not everyone is holy in the Holy Land." Watch out for pickpockets and never buy an "ancient" coin unless you are with an expert; counterfeiters have almost made it impossible to distinguish a real coin from a fake. That having been said, I've never had a problem shopping in the Old City. Asking vendors for a better price is always part of the fun.

If you look closely inside the Jaffa Gate, you can climb the tower and literally walk on top of the ancient walls. On the street to your right, there used to be a Christian bookstore. See if you can find it—and if you do, please go inside and support them.

---

## GATES OF THE OLD CITY

Ancient cities were actually massive stone fortresses. However, like a chain, a fortress is only as strong as its weakest point. In times of war, enemy forces often concentrated their attacks on the gates, typically the weakest part of the city wall. Because of this, the gates usually included or were flanked by defensive guard towers.

As we mentioned earlier, the **Jaffa Gate** on the western side of the city walls is named for the road that leads from the gate to the port city of Jaffa (Joppa). Built in 1538, the Jaffa Gate is one of the main entrances into the city. Busy with pedestrians and cars, a road allows visitors to enter the Old City through a wide gap in the wall between Jaffa Gate and the Citadel. It's also the best place to catch a cab back to the hotel if you're spending your free day exploring the Old City and are too tired to walk back.

The **New Gate** on the west wall is so named because it is the newest. Clever, huh? It was built with permission of Sultan Abdul Hamid II in 1889. The gate is located near the northwestern corner of the city and leads into the Christian Quarter.

Damascus Gate with view of Old City in the background                    *Photo: Todd Bolen*

The **Damascus Gate** to the north has two nicknames. It is called the Shechem Gate by Jews, for a city by the same name that used to be outside this gate. The Arabs call it the "Gate of the Column," because of a tall pillar that once stood in this gate's plaza during the Roman and Byzantine periods. This is the busiest and most magnificent of all Jerusalem's gates. There is one large center gate originally intended for use by persons of high station, and two smaller side entrances for the rest of us.

**Herod's Gate** (also called Flowers Gate) is just east of the Damascus Gate and is the entrance into the Muslim Quarter through the northern wall. It is named after Herod the Great, and its nickname comes from the floral carvings above the gate entrance.

The **Lions' Gate**, also known as Stephen's Gate or the Sheep Gate (Nehemiah 3:1,32; 12:39), is located on the east wall, north of the Temple Mount and today leads to the Via Dolorosa. Near the gate's crest are four figures of lions, two on the left and two on the right. It is referred to as Stephen's Gate because tradition says that the first Christian martyr was stoned outside this gate. Israeli paratroopers from the 55th Paratroop Brigade came through this gate during the Six-Day War and unfurled the Israeli flag above the Temple Mount.

*Clockwise from top left:* Dung Gate, Herod's Gate, New Gate *Lower left:* Lions' Gate (also called Stephen's Gate) *Photos: Todd Bolen*

As discussed earlier, the **East Gate** (also known as the Golden Gate or Mercy Gate) faces the Mount of Olives on the eastern side of the Old City. You can read more about the East Gate in Chapter 7.

**Dung Gate** is found in the south wall and is the gate closest to the Temple Mount. This is one of the 12 or so gates that existed at the time of Nehemiah (Nehemiah 3:14). It led out to the Valley Of Hinnom. Since the 2nd century, trash has been hauled out of the city through this gate.

**Zion Gate** is on the south wall, overlooking Mount Zion and leading to the Jewish and Armenian Quarters. This gate was used by the Israel defense forces in 1967 to enter and capture the Old City. Make sure to notice the bullet holes that can still be seen on the stones surrounding the gate.[2]

The gates of Jerusalem have seen some changes since the days of the Old Testament. To gain a better understanding of what they would have been like in biblical times, take a look at this very engaging description by Victor Knowles, founder of Peace on Earth Ministries:

> In biblical times nearly every city was a "gated" city. Strong gates were vital to the city's welfare. Gates were where business was transacted and where important announcements were made. Traders brought their goods into the city through gates. Gates were frequently the focus of enemy attacks. The weakest points of a city's walls were its gates because they were made of wood and could be set on fire. To "possess the gates" meant that you had conquered the city. See Genesis 22:17 (NASB).

> Perhaps the most famous gates in the Bible are the ten gates that were built in the wall surrounding Jerusalem. Nehemiah gave detailed attention to them (Nehemiah 3). He was distressed because the wall of Jerusalem was broken down and its gates were burned with fire (Nehemiah 1:3-4). He saw the need for a great restoration. Because of his vision and strong leadership, the job was completed in only 52 days (Nehemiah 6:15). The ten gates can symbolize the gospel story. Chapter 3 of Nehemiah starts with the **Sheep Gate**, located in the NE part of the city wall. As you might expect, this gate was where the sheep were brought into Jerusalem to be sacrificed. "All we like sheep have gone astray" (Isaiah 53:6). But Jesus, the Lamb of God, "was led as a lamb to the slaughter" (John 1:29, Isaiah 53:7). By His blood our sins are forgiven (Romans 3:25).

> Next came the **Fish Gate**. All you had to do was "follow your nose" to find this gate! Fishermen brought their catch from the Mediterranean Sea and the Jordan River through this gate. Jesus told the disciples, "I will make you fishers of men" (Mark 1:17). We are saved from our sins in order to help save others from their sins.

> The **Old Gate** is mentioned next. It was the oldest of all the gates. It

stands for the timeless principles of God's truth. Jeremiah said, "Ask for the old paths, where the good way is, and walk in it; then you find rest for your souls" (Jeremiah 6:16). We need to stay on course in the Christian life (Matt 7:14) and not veer off to some "New Gate."

The **Valley Gate** was next in line. David spoke of "the valley of the shadow of death" (Psalm 23:4). Just because we are Christians does not mean that we will not have valleys in our life. But the presence of the Shepherd will be with us; therefore, we will "fear no evil." And we will be fruitful for the best fruit is grown in the valley.

The **Refuse Gate** was another gate you could find by following your nose. Garbage and rubbish were carted through this gate to the valley of Hinnom. Sometimes it is called the Dung Gate. There are many things we should refuse for our spiritual health's sake (2 Corinthians 7:1).

The **Fountain Gate** must have been a refreshing place to visit. The Pool of Siloam graced the King's Garden. Jesus declared that from the lives of believers living water would flow. "By this He meant the Spirit" (John 7:38.39). The indwelling of the Holy Spirit in our lives will be a source of refreshment to others.

The only gate that needed no repairs was the **Water Gate**. Each gate had suffered damage because of fire, but no repairs were necessary here. Ezra set up a pulpit and taught from the Book of the Law in front of the Water Gate (Nehemiah 8:3). The Word of God cannot be destroyed and needs no revision. Today the church is cleansed "with the baptismal water by the word" (Ephesians 5:26 NTMS, Weymouth). See also Acts 2:41, Titus 3:5.

The **Horse Gate** was vital because horses were necessary to successful warfare. John saw a Rider on a white horse whose name was the Word of God (Revelation 19:11-21). War was made upon the Rider on the horse – and His army. The church is the army of Christ, engaged in spiritual warfare (Ephesians 6:10- 18). Let us "possess the gates" – even the vaunted Gates of Hades (Matthew 16:18).

The **East Gate** faced the rising sun. It was the first gate to be opened in the morning. It has been sealed up for many years but it reminds us that Jesus is coming again (Matthew 24:44). Don't be shut out when the Bridegroom comes (Matthew 25:1-13).

The **Miphkad Gate**, near the present Golden Gate, was where King David reviewed his troops and foreigners were required to register. The Hebrew word means "appointment" or "census." At the "Appointment Gate" or "Inspection Gate" we must all appear before the Judgment Seat of Christ (2 Corinthians 5:10).

*"Blessed are those who wash their robes, so that they may have the right to the tree of life, and may enter by the gates into the city"* Revelation 22:14 (NASB).[3]

## The Four Quarters

The Four Quarters of the Old City are formed along a roughly rectangular grid, but the quarters are not equal in size. To get an idea of the borders, draw a line running north to south from the Damascus Gate to the Zion Gate. Cross it with an east to west line running from the Jaffa Gate to the Lions' Gate (also called Stephen's Gate).

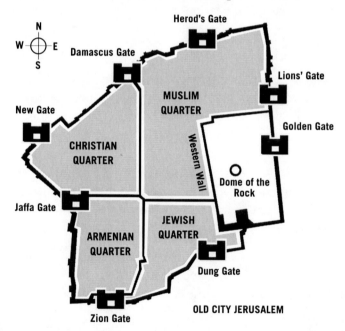

The Muslim Quarter, located in the northeastern corner, is the largest and most densely populated of the four quarters with 22,000 citizens as of 2005. Like the other three quarters of the Old City, the Muslim quarter had a mixed population of Jews as well as Muslims and Christians until the riots of 1929. Today, only 60 Jewish families live in the Muslim Quarter.

The Christian Quarter is in the northwestern corner of the Old City. Few people live in this quarter. Instead, this quarter is full of religious sites (40 holy places in all), small museums, and educational buildings. You can also find many souvenir shops, coffee shops, hotels, and restaurants. This quarter also contains the Church of the Holy Sepulchre.

First century tomb and entrance to Church of the Holy Sepulchre          *Photos: Todd Bolen*

The Armenian Quarter is the smallest of the four quarters of the Old City. Although the Armenian people are Christians, the Armenian Quarter is distinct from the Christian Quarter. Despite the small size and population of this quarter, the Armenians remain staunchly independent. Unlike most Christians in the region, they are not Arab and have chosen to stay ethnically separate. After the 1948 Arab-Israeli War, the four quarters of the city came under Jordanian control. Jordanian law required Armenians and other Christians to "give equal time to the Bible and Qur'an" in private Christian schools. Today more than 3,000 Armenians live in Jerusalem—500 of them in the Armenian Quarter.

The Jewish Quarter lies in the southeastern sector of the walled city. Jews have had a close to continuous presence here since the 8th century BC. The oldest synagogues—the Elijah the Prophet and Yohanan Ben Zakkai—are both roughly 400 years old. These synagogues are below street level, because, when they were built, Jews and Christians were not allowed to build anything higher than the Muslim structures.

In the main plaza, notice an arch that stretches skyward where one of the walls of the Hurva Synagogue once stood. Originally the Great

Synagogue, the Hurva was built in the 16th century, but was destroyed by the Ottomans. The synagogue was rebuilt in the 1850s, but was damaged in the 1948 war and then destroyed after the Jordanians took control of the Old City.

Remains of ancient Roman Cardo in the Jewish Quarter          *Photos: Todd Bolen*

The Jewish Quarter of today is built on the remains of Herod's upper city (37 BC-70 AD). The Wohl Archaeological Museum houses the underground remains of Jewish homes from the Herodian period. In 1948, Jordan forced the entire Jewish population (about 2,000 people) to leave the quarter. Ancient synagogues were destroyed and homes were sacked. The quarter remained under Jordanian control until its capture by Israeli paratroops in the Six-Day War of 1967. The quarter has since been rebuilt and settled, and has a population of 2,348 (as of 2004). Before being rebuilt, the quarter was carefully excavated under the supervision of Hebrew University archaeologist Nahman Avigad. The archaeological remains are on display in a series of museums and outdoor parks two or three stories below street level. Just off the plaza is the Cardo, a sort of ancient Byzantine super highway that ran through the heart of the city. Today, a small area is preserved with some of the original Roman columns. Just beyond the columns is an underground mall with a number of Jewish stores and art galleries. This is a good place to purchase souvenirs and, as mentioned earlier, haggling is expected.[4]

## WESTERN WALL

Built in the 1st century by Herod the Great as part of the Temple Mount complex, the Western Wall commonly refers to a 187-foot section of ancient wall on the western side of the Temple Mount. Here are some quick facts about its dimensions and composition:

- The above-ground portion of this limestone retaining wall actually spans 1,600 feet, but it is mostly hidden behind buildings that run along its length.

- At the Western Wall Plaza, the total height of the Wall from its foundation is estimated at 105 feet, with its exposed section standing approximately 62 feet high. The plaza was designated as an area for prayer when Israel captured the Old City in 1967.

- The Wall consists of 45 stone layers, 28 of them above ground and 17 underground. The first seven layers, which you can count from the ground up, date back to Herod.

- Most of the stones weigh between two and eight tons each. One giant stone located in the northern section of Wilson's Arch measures 42 feet and weighs approximately 570 tons.

Prayers wedged into cracks and Western Wall today (women's area on right)   *Photos: Todd Bolen*

When Rome destroyed the Second Temple in 70 AD, only one outer wall remained standing. The Romans probably would have destroyed this wall along with the others, but it probably didn't seem worth the effort since it was not considered part of the Temple itself; it was just an outer wall surrounding the Temple Mount. For the Jews, however, this remnant of what was their most sacred building quickly became the holiest place in Jewish life.

Throughout the centuries, Jews from all over the world have made the difficult pilgrimage to Palestine, heading immediately for the Western Wall to thank God, offer prayers, and mourn the destruction of their temple. The prayers spoken at the Wall were so intense that Gentiles began calling the site the "Wailing Wall." However, this term is considered derogatory to most Jewish people, as it refers to their audible lamentations about the temple's destruction and other hardships.[5] Let's show them honor and respect by calling the site the "Western Wall."

The Western Wall is also the holiest place still accessible to Jewish people today, because Muslims control the Temple Mount. Here, Jews are as close as they can get to the Foundation Stone, which is the rock referred to in the Dome of the Rock. Jews believe the Holy of Holies sat on this rock and that the Ark of the Covenant once rested here (Exodus 26:33). Because of the profound reverence they possess, most Jews will not set foot on the Temple Mount.

At times tens of thousands of people gather here for prayer. Most people know that you are supposed to write a prayer on a piece of paper and tuck it into a crevice in the Wall. What most people don't know is why. How did this tradition get started? In the 1700s, a desperately poor man could no longer feed his family and came to see Rabbi Chaim Ibn Attar. The rabbi wrote on some parchment and told the man to put it between the holy stones of the Western Wall. That must have worked, because 300 years later all kinds of people—from Popes to politicians to pop stars—are still putting their paper prayers in the Wall!

Today the Western Wall has gone high tech. The Israeli Telephone Company established a fax service where petitioners can send notes to be placed in the Western Wall. A number of charitable websites now offer the same service, and since July 2009, you can even "Tweet" a prayer to the Western Wall.

Not everyone is thrilled with the increased activity at the Western Wall. Some ultra-orthodox Jews believe that the custom of placing paper prayers in the crevices violates the holiness of the Wall. They believe our unholy hands should not touch any part of the Wall and that leaning against it or using it for shade diminishes its sanctity. Even using its cavities for resting prayer books or candles is frowned upon. At one point in the Wall's history, pilgrims would place nails in the cracks and paint their Hebrew names on the Wall. These practices stopped after rabbinic consensus determined that they were a desecration of holiness.

Years ago, it was not uncommon for tourists to remove a chip from the Wall or some of the sand from between its cracks as a good luck charm or memento. Some rabbis claimed this practice was "an evil custom which is totally forbidden." However, it is permissible to take twigs from the vegetation that grows in the Wall, as they contain no holiness.

Even cleaning the stones creates a problem. If placing your finger in a crevice is a no-no, according to their reading of Jewish law, scrubbing it down would be out of the question. As a result, offensive graffiti once sprayed by a tourist was left for months until it began to naturally peel away.

In the past, ultra-orthodox Jews violently broke up any prayer service organized by women. Today, there is a sectioned-off area for women only. As a sign of respect, men and married women are expected to cover their heads when approaching the Wall and to dress modestly. On Saturdays, it is forbidden to enter the area with electronic devices, including cameras, which infringe on the sanctity of the Sabbath.

Remember when leaving, the custom is to walk backwards away from the Wall. While here, make your way up the stairs behind the entrance of the Wall to one of the rooftop lookouts above. This offers the best view. From here you can see the entire Wall and the Dome of the Rock peeking from behind it.

The Western Wall is open 24 hours a day. If you can, try to see it at night when it's the most peaceful. Walk up to the Wall and feel the rough texture of thousands of battles; hear the echoes of millennia of prayers; see the honey yellow glow of past civilizations. Then step back and take in the history and majesty of this simple wall of stone. To stand and pray here is a humbling and awesome experience. For those who have never been, the Western Wall can be viewed online through a live video feed with frequently updated photos daily. Check out www.aish.com/wallcam or www.thewall.org.

**POINTS FROM THE PASTOR**

Here's an interesting and moving bit of history for you:

After Jordan captured the Western Wall and the Old City during the 1948 Arab-Israeli War, Article VIII of the 1949 Armistice Agreement allowed Israeli/Jewish access to the Western Wall. However, Jordan refused to keep its word, and Jews were effectively barred. For the next 20 years, a vantage point on Mount Zion that overlooked the Wall became the place where Jews gathered to pray.

The Western Wall came under Israeli control after Israel's Six-Day War victory in 1967. Yitzchak Rabin, fifth Prime Minister of Israel, described the moment Israeli soldiers reached the Wall:

"There was one moment in the Six-Day War which symbolized the great victory: that was the moment in which the first paratroopers—under Gur's command—reached the stones of the Western Wall, feeling the emotion of the place; there never was, and never will be, another moment like it. Nobody staged that moment. Nobody planned it in advance. Nobody prepared it and nobody was prepared for it; it was as if Providence had directed the whole thing: the paratroopers weeping—loudly and in pain—over their comrades who had fallen along the way, the words of the Kaddish prayer heard by Western Wall's stones after 19 years of silence, tears of mourning, shouts of joy, and the singing of 'Hatikvah.'"

Forty-eight hours after capturing the Wall, the military demolished the entire Moroccan Quarter, which stood just 12 feet from the Wall. Chaim Herzog, who later became Israel's sixth president, took much of the credit for the destruction of the neighborhood:

"When we visited the Wailing Wall we found a toilet attached to it...we decided to remove it and from this we came to the conclusion that we could evacuate the entire area in front of the Wailing Wall...a historical opportunity that will never return...We knew that the following Saturday, June 14, would be the Jewish festival of Shavouot and that many will want to come to pray...it all had to be completed by then."

Before demolition, the 1300-square foot area could accommodate a maximum of 12,000 people per day; after demolition it became an enormous plaza covering more than 200,000 square feet, which can now hold more than 400,000. Jews believe that the Western Wall is close to the Holy of Holies and so they come here to pray.

Rabbi Jacob Ettlinger writes, "…since the gate of heaven is near the Western Wall, it is understandable that all Israel's prayers ascend on high there…" [6]

## WESTERN WALL TUNNEL (RABBI'S TUNNEL)

While the above-ground portion of the Western Wall is close to 200 feet long, most of its original 1600-foot length is hidden beneath the Prayer Plaza and the rest of the Old City. Rabbi's Tunnel gives special access to this subterranean section of the Wall. The tunnel is underground and adjacent to the Western Wall, allowing access to the rest of the structure.

British researchers began excavating the Western Wall in the mid-1800s; however, the Six-Day War in 1967 provided an opportunity to expand the dig. The Ministry of Religious Affairs of Israel aimed to expose the continuation of the Western Wall. Lasting almost 20 years, the excavation revealed many previously unknown facts about the history and geography of the Temple Mount. A difficult endeavor, since the tunnels ran beneath residential neighborhoods constructed on top of ancient structures from the Second Temple Period, the dig was conducted with the supervision of scientific and rabbinic experts—hence the name, "Rabbi's Tunnel." Then in 1988, the Western Wall Heritage Foundation was formed and took over the excavation, maintenance, and renovations of the Western Wall and Western Wall Plaza. [7]

"Warren's Gate" lies about 150 feet into the tunnel. This sealed-off entrance has been turned into a small synagogue called "The Cave," and has become a most-sacred spot to the Jewish people. Why put a synagogue here? As mentioned earlier, assuming it was located at the traditional site under the Dome of the Rock, this is the closest Jews can get to the Holy of Holies.

The biggest stone in the Western Wall, often called the Western Stone, can be seen within the tunnel. At 44 feet long, 11 to 14 feet wide, and  weighing 570 tons, it ranks as one of the heaviest objects ever lifted by human beings without powered machinery. Make sure your guide points this stone out to you.

Western Stone                    *Photo: Todd Bolen*

Originally, tourists walking through the tunnel had to retrace their steps back to the entrance. But in 1996, Prime Minister Binyamin Netanyahu ordered a new exit to be cut into the Struthion Pool area to the Via Dolorosa nearby. Since then, large numbers of tourists are able to enter the tunnel's southern entrance near the Western Wall, walk the tunnel's length with a tour guide, and exit from the northern end. At the end of the tour the route back to the Jewish Quarter passes through the Muslim Quarter. As a precaution, sometimes Israeli soldiers accompany tourists back to the Jewish Quarter.[8]

POINTS FROM THE PASTOR

Towards the northern end of the tunnel, you'll come across a section to the left with a pool, and to the right you'll see the Roman road that ran along the outside of the temple. Oftentimes one wonders if Jesus actually traveled down this particular section. It is my belief that He most definitely would have walked by this pool with His disciples and perhaps leaned against the rail and spent time with His followers, teaching them.

This is one of the places in Israel that give me the chills when I consider that I'm actually walking where Jesus walked. But remember, in Christ's day, it wasn't a tunnel. Enjoy!

## Hezekiah's Tunnel

During the reign of Hezekiah, the king of Judah between 715 and 686 BC, another extraordinary tunnel was dug underneath the City of David in Jerusalem. It was used to bring water from the Gihon Spring on one side of the city to the other during times of war, which proved to be of immense value during the siege by the Assyrians in the 8th century BC. In his book, *Devotional Treasures from the Holy Land*, Dr. John DeLancey beautifully describes the background and discovery of Hezekiah's Tunnel. Take a look:

In 1830, a hexagonal clay prism, known as the "Taylor Prism," was discovered among the ruins of Nineveh. It tells us that Sennacherib, the king of Assyria in the Eighth Century BC, had Hezekiah trapped in Jerusalem like a "bird in a cage." Hezekiah and his engineers refortified the city walls and carved a 1,720 foot tunnel  out of solid bedrock to bring the ever-flowing waters of the Gihon spring into the inner sections of the city (1 Kings 1:38, 45; 2 Kings 20; 2 Chronicles 29-32). The carving of the tunnel was a remarkable feat!

Hezekiah's Tunnel          *Photo: Todd Bolen*

With a flashlight in hand, you can walk through this tunnel today and see the very chisel marks cut into the bedrock. An inscription found near the end of the tunnel, kept in storage at the Istanbul Museum, tells the remarkable story of how two teams chiseled toward each other until they could literally hear the sound of the other picking before breaking through.

Hezekiah's Tunnel was discovered by American explorer Edward Robinson in 1838. In the 1860s, another explorer named Charles Warren is credited for having discovered a 52 foot vertical shaft that descends to the level of the water tunnel. We can only express thanks to 19th Century explorers and archaeologists like these for dedicating their lives to this cause here in the City of David. Whether studying the story of David's capture of the city (2 Samuel 5) or how Hezekiah and his fellow citizens of Jerusalem withstood the massive Assyrian army in 701 BC, archaeology continues to shed light on how these events were achieved.

Like a royal inscription found on a piece of pottery here, God is more concerned about what is written on our heart. Often, like pottery that needs to be cleared of dirt and debris, God finds dirt and debris upon our hearts as well. It is God's Spirit who renews our spiritual walk (Titus 3:5).

Likewise, just as archaeology sheds light on the ancient past of the Bible, it is God's Spirit who reveals to the follower of Christ the pathways to God. Unlike walking through Hezekiah's Tunnel without a flashlight, God delights when we walk in the light way. God is pleased when we entrust our ways to His wisdom (Proverbs 3:5-6; Proverbs 4:6).

Thanks be to God for the light He sheds on our pathway. Like a flashlight radiating beams into the darkened tunnel of Hezekiah, God provides His Spirit for our enlightenment. God has provided the gift of illumination of His Spirit that enables us to walk through the dark tunnels of life with confidence. This requires us to put aside the "pitch darkness" of our own wisdom. Allow God's Spirit to shed light on your life.[10]

## Temple Mount

*On reaching Jerusalem, Jesus entered the temple area and began driving out those who were buying and selling there. He overturned the tables of the money changers and the benches of those selling doves, and would not allow anyone to carry merchandise through the temple courts. And as He taught them, He said, "Is it not written: 'My house will be called a house of prayer for all nations'? But you have made it a 'den of robbers.'"* Mark 11:15-17

Jewish Midrash (a large collection of rabbinical sermons that help explain the teachings of the Torah and Talmud) [11] holds that it was from the Temple Mount that the world expanded into its present form, and that this was where God gathered the dust He used to create the first man, Adam. The Torah records that it was here that God chose to rest his Divine Presence, and consequently, two Jewish Temples were built at the site. According to Jewish tradition, one day the Third Temple will be built here, and it will be the final one. Because no one today can pinpoint the exact location of the Holy of Holies, many Jews will not set foot on the Mount.

In Islam, this site is revered as the destination of Muhammad's journey to Jerusalem and the location of his ascent to heaven, although there is no record of him being there. The Temple Mount is also associated with biblical prophets who are esteemed in Islam, and it's the location of the al-Aqsa Mosque and the Dome of the Rock, the oldest Islamic structure in the world.

Dome of the Rock and al-Aqsa Mosque                    *Photos: Todd Bolen*

Often visitors wonder why the Temple Mount isn't the highest point in the city when the Bible seems to describe it as such. The answer is that the city today (including the Old City) has grown and shifted from its original location. The earliest city of Jerusalem is the "City of David," a smaller hill south of, and lower than, the Temple Mount.

## TEMPLE MOUNT IN THE BIBLE

• Abraham journeys three days from Beershiva or Garet to Mount Moriah in Jerusalem to offer his son Isaac as a sacrifice in obedience to God's command. God provides a substitute (Genesis 22; Hebrews 11:8-19). Mt. Moriah is the site of the Temple Mount.

• David returns the Ark of the Covenant to Jerusalem and places it in the Tabernacle of Moses erected there (2 Samuel 6:1-18; 1 Chronicles chapters 15 and 16). David plans the First Temple, but is not permitted to build it (2 Samuel 7:1-17).

• David purchases the threshing floor of Araunah, which later becomes the site of the First Temple, and erects an altar of sacrifice on Mt. Moriah (2 Samuel 24:1-25; 1 Chronicles 21:1-22:5).

• Solomon, with the help of Hiram of Tyre and 183,600 workers, builds the First Temple and the Royal Palace using local limestone, cedar from Lebanon, and large amounts of gold and silver. The Temple is built in seven years (1 Kings chapters 5 through 9; 2 Chronicles chapters 2 and 3).

• In 924 BC, Pharaoh Shishak of Egypt plunders the Temple and carries off much of the gold and silver (1 Kings 14:25-28; 2 Chronicles 12:1-11).

• Joash, king of Judah, repairs the Temple, establishes a maintenance fund, and brings a period of revival and reforms to the southern kingdom (2 Kings 12:4-5).

• Ahaz, king of Judah, dismantles Solomon's bronze vessels and places a private Syrian altar in the Temple (2 Kings 16:1-20; 2 Chronicles 28).

• Hezekiah, with the help of God and the prophet Isaiah, resists the Assyrian attempt to capture Jerusalem (2 Chronicles 32). He restores the Temple and brings another period of national reform and revival (2 Chronicles 29-31). Later, he strips gold from the Temple to pay tribute to Sennacherib (2 Kings 18-16).

• Josiah repairs the Temple and brings about national religious reforms (2 Chronicles 34-35).

• In 586 BC, the First Temple is destroyed by Nebuchadnezzar, the Babylonian king, and the sacred vessels are carried off to Babylon. Sometime between 553-540 BC, Belshazzar of Babylon later desecrates these vessels (Daniel 5).

• Ezekiel receives a vision from God describing in detail the great Temple to be built during the reign of the Messiah in an age yet to come (Ezekiel 40-48).

• In 516 BC, Jews under Nehemiah's leadership return from Babylon in small numbers to rebuild the city and its walls (Daniel 9; Haggai 2:18-19; Nehemiah).

• The construction of the Second Temple begins around 538 BC. Despite fierce opposition and delays, it is completed under Darius of Persia in 516 BC with the erection of an altar of sacrifice on Mt. Moriah.

• In 332 BC, priests from Jerusalem meet the invading army of Alexander the Great and persuade him to not destroy Jerusalem by showing him Scriptures that predict his rise to power. After the death of Alexander in 323 BC, a series of wars between Syria and

Egypt subject the Holy Land to multiple distresses (Daniel 9:24-27; 11:1-35; Zechariah 9:1-10; writings of Josephus).

• Between 140-37 BC, the Hasmonean dynasty expands the Temple Mount. The Hasmoneans are an independent Jewish state. Evidence of a Hasmonean expansion of the Temple Mount has been recovered by archaeologist Leen Ritmeyer.

• Around 19 BC, the Temple Mount is enlarged and leveled by Herod the Great. It takes 10,000 workers, 100 priests, 1,000 wagons, and 46 years to get the job done. Herod has the area leveled by cutting away rock on the northwest side and raising the sloping ground to the south, filling in the sections with earth and rubble. Antonia Fortress and a rainwater reservoir are also built during this period of expansion. By the time Herod is done, the Temple Mount has doubled in size—covering 35 acres.

• Jesus is presented at the Temple and dedicated to God by His parents (Luke 2:21-24).

• Jesus, at age 12, talks to priests and teachers in the Second Temple while His parents are in Jerusalem for Passover (Luke 2:41-50).

• Jesus is tempted by the devil on the pinnacle of the Temple (Luke 4:9).

• Jesus casts out moneychangers from the Temple early in His ministry (John 2:13-16), and again three years later.

• During His final week of life before the resurrection, the Lord teaches in the Temple courts and confronts the crowds and Pharisees there. Jesus predicts destruction of the Second Temple (Matthew 21; Mark 11; Luke 19:41-48; John 12:12-50).

• Followers of Jesus, who are gathered in the Temple Courts 10 days later on Pentecost Sunday, experience the coming of the Spirit of God to give birth to the Church of Jesus Christ. Peter preaches to the crowds and many are saved (Acts 2).

• Stephen is martyred on the Temple Mount; Saul of Tarsus is present (Acts 6-7).

• James, brother of Jesus and leader of the Church in Jerusalem, is martyred by being thrown from the pinnacle of the Temple Mount.[12]

• Titus, son of Roman Emperor Vespasian, destroys the Temple Mount and pretty much all of Jerusalem in 70 AD.

• Constantine's mother, Helena, built a small church on the Mount in the 4th century AD. The church was later destroyed and the Dome of the Rock was built on its ruins between 689 and 691 AD. (More on the Dome of the Rock in the next section.)[13]

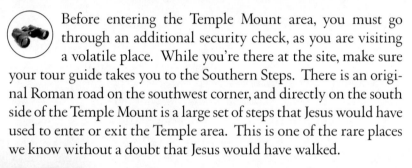 Before entering the Temple Mount area, you must go through an additional security check, as you are visiting a volatile place. While you're there at the site, make sure your tour guide takes you to the Southern Steps. There is an original Roman road on the southwest corner, and directly on the south side of the Temple Mount is a large set of steps that Jesus would have used to enter or exit the Temple area. This is one of the rare places we know without a doubt that Jesus would have walked.

 If you have time, go sit on the Southern Steps, look at the size of the Temple Mount wall, and imagine Jesus walking down these steps with His disciples as the following scene unfolds:

*As he was leaving the temple, one of his disciples said to him, "Look, Teacher! What massive stones! What magnificent buildings!" "Do you see all these great buildings?" replied Jesus. "Not one stone here will be left on another; every one will be thrown down." As Jesus was sitting on the Mount of Olives opposite the temple, Peter, James, John and Andrew asked him privately, "Tell us, when will these things happen? And what will be the sign that they are all about to be fulfilled?" Jesus said to them: "Watch out that no one deceives you. Many will come in my name, claiming, 'I am he,' and will deceive many. When you hear of wars and rumors of wars, do not be alarmed. Such things must happen, but the end is still to come. Nation will rise against nation, and kingdom against kingdom. There will be earthquakes in various places, and famines. These are the beginning of birth pains. "You must be*

*on your guard. You will be handed over to the local councils and flogged in the synagogues. On account of me you will stand before governors and kings as witnesses to them. And the Gospel must first be preached to all nations. Whenever you are arrested and brought to trial, do not worry beforehand about what to say. Just say whatever is given you at the time, for it is not you speaking, but the Holy Spirit. "Brother will betray brother to death, and a father his child. Children will rebel against their parents and have them put to death. All men will hate you because of me, but he who stands firm to the end will be saved."* Mark 13: 1-13

## DOME OF THE ROCK

Standing where the First and Second Temples once stood, the incandescent golden Dome of the Rock is impossible to miss as it dominates the Jerusalem skyline. This octagon-shaped monument was built by the Muslim ruler Abd al Malik in 688-691 AD. Today, most scholars believe that the Dome of the Rock sits upon the location of the Holy of Holies, as well as the Foundation Stone—the name of the rock upon which the Ark of the Covenant was placed in the First Temple. During the Second Temple period when the Ark of the Covenant had been hidden, the stone was used by the High Priest who offered up incense and sprinkled the blood of the sacrifices on it during the Yom Kippur service. [14] The rock, 30 feet by 24 feet, currently "occupies the center of the shrine and is surrounded by lavish décor, stained glass windows, pillars of marble, [and] glass partitions [to] keep souvenir hunters from temptation!"[15] Muslims, who today control the Temple Mount by Israel's permission, will not allow archeologists to work the site. Until the site can be excavated, the exact location of the Foundation Stone can't be known.

The Dome of the Rock was badly rattled during an earthquake on July 11, 1927. In 1955 Jordan, with funds from Arab governments and Turkey, began a massive renovation on the monument. As part of this facelift, the dome was covered with a durable aluminum and bronze alloy. The restoration was completed in August 1964, but in 1998 King Hussein of Jordan decided to give the dome a serious upgrade, covering it in 176 pounds of 24-karat gold leaf that cost $8.2 million dollars.

Under Jordanian rule, Jews were forbidden from entering the Old City, but after the 1967 Six-Day War, Israel regained control of Jerusalem and the Dome of the Rock. Within hours Rabbi Shlomo Goren entered the Dome of the Rock with a Torah book and a shofar.

Sadly, just a few hours after the Israeli flag was hoisted over the Dome of the Rock General Moshe Dayan, in attempt to keep the peace, ordered that it be lowered. A few days after the war was over, 200,000 Jews flocked to the Temple Mount and Western Wall in the first mass Jewish pilgrimage since the destruction of Temple in 70 AD. What a homecoming that must have been!

Surrounded by angry Muslim/Arab neighbors, the Israeli government decided to let the Islamic Wakf (or trust) control the site, although it remains under Israeli sovereignty. Today, Jews are generally banned from praying on the Mount or doing anything that might disturb Muslims. However, recently the police have been allowing religious Jews to let their tzitzit (tassels) hang freely outside their clothing. At times, the police have even allowed for very limited Jewish prayer; for example, during the 2008-09 Gaza War, a small number of Jews were allowed to pray atop the Mount for the welfare of the Israeli Defense Forces.

In 2006, the compound was finally reopened to non-Muslims visitors free of charge. Non-Muslims may never enter on Fridays, Saturdays, or Muslim holidays. Entry is through a covered wooden walkway next to the security entrance to the Western Wall known as the Mugrabi or Maimonides Gate. Non-Muslims are not allowed to enter the mosques, and visitors must undergo a strict security screening. Items such as Hebrew prayer books or musical instruments are not allowed.

You may wonder why Jews continue to allow these restrictions to be placed on them by the Muslim Council. First, as one Jewish tour guide once explained to us, keeping the peace is of the utmost importance to Israelis. The second reason goes clear back to the Old Testament. Only the High Priest could enter the Holy of Holies and the penalty for breaking this law was death. Since the exact location of the Holy of Holies is unknown most Orthodox Jews consider stepping on the Mount to be forbidden.

For Muslims, the Dome of the Rock and al-Aqsa Mosque make Jerusalem the third-holiest city, after Mecca and Medina. Muslims teach that this is where Abraham nearly sacrificed his son Ishmael and where Muhammad ascended to heaven, which is a major biblical rewrite. Scripture teaches that this is where Abraham nearly sacrificed his son Isaac (Genesis 22:2) and where the future Messiah will return (Ezekiel 43:7).

Muslims, however, deny the Sonship and deity of Jesus and teach that He is just a prophet. These beliefs are clearly on display inside the mosque. Five times the Qur'anic verse that reads "God has no companion" is repeated along with this remarkable prayer, "In the name of the One God (Allah) Pray for your Prophet and Servant Jesus son of Mary." Building the mosque on this particular site was no accident, for the Lie stands as close to the Truth as it can, making it easy to confuse the two: Ishmael and his descendants become the sons of the promise instead of the sons of the law; Jesus becomes a prophet instead of the very Son of God; and Muhammad ascends to heaven from here instead of the resurrected Savior.[16]

Despite deception and confusion, we have this blessed assurance of our Heavenly Father's ultimate plan, found in Philippians 2:9-11: *Therefore God exalted him to the highest place and gave him the name that is above every name, that at the name of Jesus every knee should bow, in heaven and on earth and under the earth, and every tongue acknowledge that Jesus Christ is Lord, to the glory of God the Father.*

## AL-AQSA MOSQUE

More important to the Muslims than the Dome of the Rock is al-Aqsa Mosque. The mosque is the third most holy place in the Muslim world, after the shrines in Mecca and Medina (both of which are in Saudi Arabia). The original mosque was built between 705 and 715 AD, but it has been destroyed and rebuilt many times.

The al-Aqsa Mosque is on the Temple Mount where Solomon built the first permanent Jewish temple. According to Jewish tradition, Solomon's Temple housed the Ark of the Covenant and the Ten Commandments. The Temple also became the only legal place to make sacrifices.

Al-Aqsa was originally a small prayer house and was later expanded. It was completely destroyed by earthquakes in 746 and 1033 AD. The mosque standing today was built in 1035 AD. In 1099, the Crusaders captured Jerusalem and for a short time they used the mosque as a church and a palace. In 1187 AD, under Islamic Crusader Saladin, al-Aqsa became a mosque once more.

The site is like a lightning rod for disasters. There is a history of earthquakes dating back to 31 BC. In fact, the Dead Sea Rift runs directly under the Temple Mount and Zechariah prophesies that the Mount of Olives will one day be split in half by an earthquake (Zechariah 14:4). There were major earthquakes here in 1927 and 1937, which seriously damaged the mosque. In 1969, King Abdullah of Jordan was assassinated here, and a fire gutted the southeastern wing of the mosque in the same year. At first, Palestinians and Israelis blamed each other for the fire, both turned out to be wrong. The fire was actually started by Michael Dennis Rohan, an Australian tourist who was a member of the Worldwide Church of God sect. He hoped that by burning down al-Aqsa Mosque he would hasten the Second Coming of Jesus, making way for the rebuilding of the Jewish Temple on the Temple Mount. Rohan was put in a mental institution, found to be insane, and was later deported from Israel.[17]

POINTS FROM THE PASTOR

In all honesty, I struggle every time I go up to the Temple Mount area and see the Dome of the Rock and the al-Aqsa Mosque. On one hand, it is so peaceful and beautiful up there, and yet it seems so wrong that the Jewish people do not have full access to the Temple Mount. I struggle with understanding how this was ever allowed, yet I confess I do not understand all the complexities of the Israeli-Arab conflict. For the sake of peace, I suppose, it is acceptable. I also believe that if the Jewish state ever removed the Dome of the Rock or the mosque, it would be the beginning of the end...perhaps World War III.

In the depths of my heart, I believe God is ultimately in control; He will return in the blinking of an eye, and all things will be settled. May we once again take some time on this holy site and pray to the One true God and for the peace of Jerusalem.

## SAINT ANNE'S CRUSADER CHURCH

To honor one's parents is near the top of the list of God's commands
(Exodus 20:12), and the Church of Saint Anne does not fall short in this
regard. The beautiful 12th century Crusader church was built to commemorate Mary's parents, Joachim and Anne (Hannah), who are said
to have been living in Jerusalem during the time of Mary's birth. It
was erected between 1131 and 1138 AD to replace a previous Byzantine
church. You may want to stop here before embarking on the Via Dolorosa, since the church is near the beginning of the First Station.

Unlike other Crusader churches, St. Anne's escaped destruction under Muslim rule in the 12th century because it was converted to an
Islamic seminary. If you read Arabic you can still see Saladin's name
inscribed above the doorway. Eventually abandoned, the church fell
into ruin until the Ottomans donated it to France in 1856. Though
the church has been restored; most of what remains today is original.

Exterior and interior views of St. Anne's Crusader Church        *Photos: Todd Bolen*

The church is right next to the Bethesda Pool, which is believed to be
the site where Jesus healed a paralytic (John 5:1-15). You can also see
ruins of a Roman temple to the god of medicine, as well as the remains
of a Byzantine church that was built over the temple.

With a garden surrounding the church in full bloom in spring and
summer, songbirds, and candles burning softly, St. Anne's Church
has an undeniably gentle and welcoming atmosphere. The simplic-
ity both inside and outside of the church sets it apart from all others.
You may notice that the building leans slightly to the side. Some tour
guides claim the tilt is symbolic of Jesus on the cross. I suspect the
builder just needed a level.

St. Anne's acoustics are so perfect that pilgrim groups come to sing in the church throughout the day. You, too, are welcome to sing but remember only religious songs are permitted. So, just to review, "Awesome God" and "Amazing Grace" would be excellent choices; "My Girl" and "Heartbreak Hotel," not so much. Please be respectful to the other groups trying to enter and exit. You may feel compelled to linger and enjoy the sweet sound of voices lifted up to the Lord, but try to limit your time inside the chapel out of consideration of others.[18]

## POOL OF BETHESDA

Bethesda is a series of ancient pools in the Muslim Quarter of Jerusalem. Its name can be translated "house of mercy" in Aramaic; and since the 4th century, it has also been called the Sheep Pool, which came from a misunderstanding. The Gospel of John describes the pool's location using the Greek word probatike,

Pool of Bethesda                    Photo: Todd Bolen

which means, "pertaining to sheep." Eusebius, an early 4th century Christian, interpreted this as "the sheep-pool" and it stuck. Today scholars think the word, probatike, actually referred to Bethesda's location near the Sheep Gate.

Surrounded by five pillars or columns, the pools are fed by a nearby spring. John 5:4 asserts that an angel moved the waters at certain times and healed the sick. It was here at the Pool of Bethesda that Jesus healed the man who had been lame for 38 years. Though there was some doubt regarding the actual existence of this pool, an archaeological discovery in the 19th century confirmed the historical accuracy of the biblical account. Then in 1964, further archaeological excavation revealed the remains of the Byzantine and Crusader churches, Hadrian's Temple of Asclepius and Serapis, the small healing pools of the Asclepieion, the other of the two large pools, and the dam between them. These reservoirs supplied water to the Temple Mount during the time of the First Temple, and is referenced in the Old Testament as the "Upper Pool." [19]

## THE POOL OF BETHESDA IN THE BIBLE

Seen here as the "Upper Pool," the Pool of Bethesda is referenced within these three Scriptures in the Old Testament:

*The king of Assyria sent his supreme commander, his chief officer and his field commander with a large army, from Lachish to King Hezekiah at Jerusalem. They came up to Jerusalem and stopped at the aqueduct of the Upper Pool, on the road to the Washerman's Field.* 2 Kings 18:17

*Then the king of Assyria sent his field commander with a large army from Lachish to King Hezekiah at Jerusalem. When the commander stopped at the aqueduct of the Upper Pool, on the road to the Launderer's Field...*
Isaiah 36:2

*Then the LORD said to Isaiah, "Go out, you and your son Shear-Jashub, to meet Ahaz at the end of the aqueduct of the Upper Pool, on the road to the Launderer's Field."* Isaiah 7:3

And here is John's well-known account of Christ healing the lame man at the Pool of Bethesda:

*Some time later, Jesus went up to Jerusalem for one of the Jewish festivals. Now there is in Jerusalem near the Sheep Gate a pool, which in Aramaic is called Bethesda and which is surrounded by five covered colonnades. Here a great number of disabled people used to lie—the blind, the lame, the paralyzed. One who was there had been an invalid for thirty-eight years. When Jesus saw him lying there and learned that he had been in this condition for a long time, he asked him, "Do you want to get well?" "Sir," the invalid replied, "I have no one to help me into the pool when the water is stirred. While I am trying to get in, someone else goes down ahead of me." Then Jesus said to him, "Get up! Pick up your mat and walk." At once the man was cured; he picked up his mat and walked. The day on which this took place was a Sabbath...*
John 5:1-9

**POINTS FROM THE PASTOR**

Throughout the New Testament, Jesus performed many miracles. Oftentimes, the purpose of these miracles was to bring validation that He was indeed the Son of God, the Christ, the Chosen One. Other times, He performed miracles out of His compassion, love, and concern for others—as in the feeding of 5,000 or raising His friend Lazarus from the dead.

The problem is that many folks began following Jesus just because of the wonder and awe of the miracles, instead of desiring to put their trust and faith in Him because He was the Savior of the world. Even today, there are many who seek a miracle of healing or deliverance, which Jesus is able to perform when it's in accordance with His will. However, my prayer is that your faith in Jesus Christ is not contingent upon whether or not He performs a miracle in your life. I pray you will study His life and His teachings, and read the testimony of those who followed Him, earnestly seeking out if He is, in fact, God's one and only Son. The greatest miracle of all is not a matter of health or finances; the greatest miracle of all is the miracle of salvation that is promised to all who believe:

*For God so loved the world that he gave his one and only Son, that whoever believes in him shall not perish but have eternal life. For God did not send his Son into the world to condemn the world, but to save the world through him.* John 3:16-17

---

## Church of the Holy Sepulchre

*Two other men, both criminals, were also led out with him to be executed. When they came to the place called the Skull, there they crucified him, along with the criminals – one on his right, the other on his left. Jesus said, "Father, forgive them, for they do not know what they are doing." And they divided up his clothes by casting lots.* Luke 23:32-34

After Roman Emperor Constantine converted to Christianity, he took an interest in the holy places associated with his newfound faith and commissioned many churches to be constructed throughout the Holy Land. One of these churches was the Church of the Holy Sepulchre, which Constantine began building in about 326 AD by leveling a pagan temple to the goddess Aphrodite. Today, the site is revered by Christians as the hill of Calvary (Golgotha) where Jesus was crucified and buried.

In 614 AD, the Church of the Holy Sepulchre ("tomb") was severely damaged by fire when the Persians invaded Jerusalem and captured the cross. But in 630, Roman (Byzantine) Emperor Heraclius marched triumphantly into Jerusalem, restored the cross, and rebuilt the church.

Christians were forced to surrender Jerusalem to Muslim control under caliph Omar in 638. The Church of the Holy Sepulchre continued to function as a Christian church under the benevolent protection of Omar and early Muslim rulers, but this changed on October 18, 1009, when the "mad" Fatimid caliph Hakim had wrecking crews systematically destroy the church. Ironically, if Omar had turned the church into a mosque, Hakim probably would have left it alone.

Though Jerusalem's Christian community could not afford the repairs, the Church of the Holy Sepulchre was finally rebuilt in 1048 when Emperor Constantine IX Monomachos and Patriarch Nicephorus of Constantinople financed the reconstruction. The funds, however, were not adequate to completely restore the original church; the atrium and the basilica were completely lost and only the courtyard and the rotunda remained.

Exterior and interior view of the Church of the Holy Sepulchre          *Photos: Todd Bolen*

In 1112, the Crusaders began to slowly renovate the church, building a monastery where the Constantinian basilica used to be and replacing the shrine of Christ's tomb in 1119. The Constantinian courtyard was covered with a Romanesque church (dedicated in 1149), which was connected to the rotunda by a great arched opening. A bell tower was added in 1170.

Subsequent centuries were not very kind to the church, which suffered damage, desecration, and neglect. The Franciscans conducted a significant renovation in 1555, but attempts at repair often did more damage than good. A fire in 1808 and an earthquake in 1927 also did extensive damage.

Then, in 1959, the Latin, Greek, and Armenian communities agreed on a major renovation plan. They vowed to replace only the elements that were incapable of fulfilling their structural function. Local masons were trained to trim stone in the style of the 11th century for the rotunda and in the 12th century style for the church. With all the additions, Constantine's church was much larger than the one that stands today, though it had a simpler layout.

There are three primary custodians of the Church of the Holy Sepulchre, first appointed when the Crusaders held Jerusalem: the Greek Orthodox, the Armenian Apostolic, and the Roman Catholic churches. In the 1800s, the Coptic Orthodox, the Ethiopian Orthodox, and the Syrian Orthodox acquired lesser responsibilities. An agreement regulates times and places of worship for each church; however, it has not kept them from fighting.

For example, a brawl broke out between the Coptics and the Ethiopians in the summer of 2002, and 11 people were hospitalized. Another incident occurred in 2004 during Orthodox celebrations of the Exaltation of the Holy Cross—a fistfight broke out when a door to the Franciscan chapel was left open and taken as a sign of disrespect. On Palm Sunday in April 2008, a fight erupted when a Greek monk was ejected from the building by a rival faction. Another clash occurred between Armenian and Greek monks in November 2008 during celebrations for the Feast of the Holy Cross. And these are just the most recent skirmishes!

Since such violence among the communities breaks out from time to time, perhaps it's good that none of them controls the main entrance to the church. In 1192, Saladin assigned this responsibility to two neighboring Muslim families. The Joudeh were entrusted with the key; the Nusseibeh (custodians of the church since the days of Caliph Omar in 637 and the oldest Arab family in Jerusalem) retained the position of keeping the door. This arrangement remains in modern times. Twice each day, a Joudeh family member brings the key to the door, which is then locked and unlocked by a Nusseibeh.

The Church of the Holy Sepulchre has been an important pilgrimage destination since the 4th century and is still one of the holiest Christian sites in the world. Think about it—the nails, the cross, the soldiers casting lots for Jesus' garments, the thieves on either side of Him, the cry "Father, forgive them," the sword-pierced side, the excruciating death, the earthquake, the darkened sky—it all very likely happened here.

Not all historians and archaeologists agree, but for centuries many have held the belief that this church was built over the actual tomb of Christ. Here is some of the supporting evidence:

- The site was outside of the city walls at the time of Jesus' death.

- Tombs from the 1st century are preserved inside the church.

- Christians held services at this site until 66 AD.

- Even after the area was brought inside the city walls in 41-43 AD, the locals did not build here.

- In 135 AD, Roman Emperor Hadrian built the Temple of Venus (Aphrodite) on the site. If Christians believed the site was holy, he might have done this to prove that Roman gods were more powerful than the God of Christianity.

- In the early 300s, Constantine built his church here, which was an inconvenient and impractical site. Why go to the trouble of tearing down the massive Temple of Venus—when there was an open space nearby—unless tradition clearly stated this was where Jesus died and was buried?

- Historian Eusebius claimed that under the torn-down Temple of Venus, the original memorial was found. [20]

Based on the above factors, the Oxford Archaeological Guide to the Holy Land has concluded that this is "very probably" the place where Jesus Christ died and was buried. Israeli scholar Dan Bahat, former City Archaeologist of Jerusalem, said this:

"We may not be absolutely certain that the site of the Holy Sepulchre Church is the site of Jesus' burial, but we have no other site that can lay a claim nearly as weighty, and we really have no reason to reject the authenticity of the site."[21]

I'm not completely convinced that this is the place where Jesus died and was buried—as you will see when we visit the Garden Tomb in the last chapter of this book—but who's to know for sure? Once you get to the Garden Tomb, you'll have a completely different experience. You'll actually see a place that still looks like "the place of the Skull" today.

POINTS FROM THE PASTOR

While the staunch, religious ceremony that is so prevalent in the Church of the Holy Sepulchre gives me an uneasy feeling, I get an opposite feeling—one of peace and tranquility—at the Garden Tomb. Don't make your decision until you've visited both places. Either way, may we never forget that Jesus Christ died so that we would have life:

*But God demonstrates his own love for us in this: While we were still sinners, Christ died for us.* Romans 5:8

## VIA DOLOROSA

*As the soldiers led him away, they seized Simon from Cyrene, who was on his way in from the country, and put the cross on him and made him carry it behind Jesus. A large number of people followed him, including women who mourned and wailed for him. Jesus turned and said to them, "Daughters of Jerusalem, do not weep for me; weep for yourselves and for your children. For the time will come when you will say, 'Blessed are the childless women, the wombs that never bore and the breasts that never nursed!' Then they will say to the mountains, "Fall on us!" and to the hills, "Cover us!"' For if people do these things when the tree is green, what will happen when it is dry?"*
Luke 23:26-31

The Via Dolorosa, which means the Way of Suffering, is a street within the Old City of Jerusalem. Since the 18th century, it has been held to be the path that Jesus walked, carrying His cross, on the way to His crucifixion. Along the Via Dolorosa are the nine Stations of the Cross; the remaining five stations are inside the Church of the Holy Sepulchre.

During the Byzantine era, a Holy Thursday procession started from the top of the Mount of Olives, stopped in Gethsemane, entered the Old City at the Lions' Gate, and followed approximately the same route to the Church of the Holy Sepulchre that the Via Dolorosa follows today. The route has always been debated. Some claim the eastern hill route, while others argue for the western hill route. In the 18th century, they finally settled on the eastern route, but it turns out they may have been wrong.

The belief that the Via Dolorosa was the biblical route was based on the assumption that the Praetorium—the place where Jesus was condemned by Pontius Pilate (Matthew 27:27 and Mark 15:16)—was next to the Antonia Fortress. Josephus records that the Roman governors stayed in Herod's palace when they were in Jerusalem, carried out their judgments on the pavement immediately outside it, and had those found guilty flogged there. Josephus' writings place Herod's palace on the western hill. In 2001, under a corner of the Jaffa Gate citadel, which is on the western hill, part of Herod's palace was uncovered.

Ultimately, which road Jesus took doesn't really matter. What matters is that He took that road for us.

Today, the traditional route starts just inside the Lions' Gate (St. Stephen's Gate) at the Umariya Elementary School, near the location of the former Antonia Fortress, and makes its way westward through the Old City to the Church of the Holy Sepulchre. The stations are as follows:

**First Station** – Highlights the biblical account of the trial and scourging of Jesus. The Church of the Flagellation commemorates this with three stained glass windows. Don't miss the mosaic crown of thorns inside the dome.

**Second Station** – Focuses on Pontius Pilate's speech in John 19:5-15. Jesus was robed in purple, crowned with thorns, mocked, and here He took up His cross.

**Third Station** – Commemorates Jesus' first fall while carrying the cross.

Although not mentioned in the Bible, Catholic tradition says that Jesus stumbled three times on His way to the cross.

**Fourth Station** – Memorializes where Jesus passed Mary on the way to the cross. The New Testament makes no mention of this but the Church of Our Lady of the Spasm (no joke—that's the name) marks it. Make sure to notice the mosaic imprint of Mary's sandals.

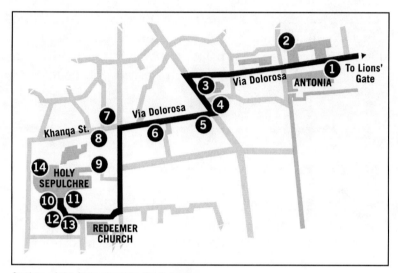

Stations of the Cross along the Via Dolorosa

**Fifth Station** – Commemorates the site where Simon of Cyrene was ordered to pick up Jesus' cross and carry it for Him. On the right side of the entrance is a rock with an indentation which some people believe Jesus made when He leaned on it.

**Sixth Station** – Focuses on yet another extra-biblical event. Tradition says that Saint Veronica lived on the Via Dolorosa. She came out to wipe Jesus' brow with a cloth and His image was left imprinted on it. The cloth has been kept at St. Peter's Basilica in Rome since the 8th century.

**Seventh Station** – Commemorates the second fall of Jesus.

**Eighth Station** – Acknowledges the events found in Luke 23:27-31 when Jesus told the Daughters of Jerusalem, "Do not weep for me; weep for yourselves and your children…" The station is marked by a stone in the wall that reads in Latin "Jesus Christ is Triumphant."

**Ninth Station** – Commemorates Jesus' third fall.

Stations 10-14 can be viewed within the Church of the Holy Sepulchre grounds and represent where Jesus was crucified, promised His kingdom to the repentant thief, entrusted Mary and John to each other, died on the cross, and where He was laid in the tomb.

Each Friday, a Roman Catholic procession walks the Via Dolorosa route, starting out at the first station. The procession is organized by the Franciscans of this monastery, who also lead the procession. Reenactments also regularly take place on the route, ranging from amateur to professional productions with historically accurate clothing and props. [22]

This may be the wrong route and there may be a lot of religious fanfare that accompanies the weekly procession, but don't let those things get in the way of what Jesus did for each and every one of us. How many of us would be unjustly accused, humiliated, spat on, whipped, and crucified for a rebellious child who wanted nothing to do with us? But that is exactly the punishment our Savior took so that we could have everlasting life with Him. You may find that you want to drop to your knees from humble gratitude that we are loved like that. Just take a look at these sweet, prophetic words from Isaiah 53:3-5:

*He was despised and rejected by mankind,*
*a man of suffering, and familiar with pain.*
*Like one from whom people hide their faces*
*he was despised, and we held him in low esteem.*
*Surely he took up our pain*
*and bore our suffering,*
*yet we considered him punished by God,*
*stricken by him, and afflicted.*
*But he was pierced for our transgressions,*
*he was crushed for our iniquities;*
*the punishment that brought us peace was on him,*
*and by his wounds we are healed.*

## Looking Forward

As we conclude our stay in Jerusalem, where we've spent much time examining her past, let's take a moment to turn our eyes to her future. While Jerusalem plays a very important role in biblical history, it will also be front and center in the fulfillment of biblical prophecy. Jesus told His disciples that He would visibly return there. In a prophecy He gave while overlooking Jerusalem from the Mount of Olives, He said:

*"Immediately after the distress of those days the sun will be darkened, and the moon will not give its light; the stars will fall from the sky, and the heavenly bodies will be shaken. Then will appear the sign of the Son of Man in heaven. And then all the peoples of the earth will mourn when they see the Son of Man coming on the clouds of heaven, with power and great glory."* Matthew 24:29-30

Where will the Lord return? The Old Testament prophet Zechariah was inspired to write:

*"A day of the LORD is coming, Jerusalem, when your possessions will be plundered and divided up within your very walls. I will gather all the nations to Jerusalem to fight against it; the city will be captured, the houses ransacked, and the women raped. Half of the city will go into exile, but the rest of the people will not be taken from the city. Then the LORD will go out and fight against those nations, as he fights on a day of battle. On that day his feet will stand on the Mount of Olives, east of Jerusalem, and the Mount of Olives will be split in two from east to west, forming a great valley, with half of the mountain moving north and half moving south."* Zechariah 14:1-4

Though we are told that Jesus could come at any time "at an hour you do not expect," we have been given instruction on how to pray until that day comes. See Psalm 122:6-9 and Matthew 6:5-13.

This ancient city has seen so much. It has seen victory and defeat, cruelty and compassion, sinfulness and salvation, the death and resurrection of Jesus. Jerusalem stands as a monument to what has been and what will be, and her story isn't finished yet. Even though our faith is not found in material objects or on plots of land, this city reminds us that our Savior walked, taught, healed, lived, died, rose again, and will one day return for His own.

JERUSALEM

*Top:* Midnight at the Western Wall.

*Center left and right:* Temple Mount during Jesus' life, Temple Mount today and Dome of the Rock.

*Above left and right:* Temple Mount walls during Jesus' life and area called Robinson's Arch today.

*Right:* Archway over start of Via Dolorosa.

*Photos: Steve Beaumont*

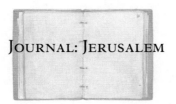

# JOURNAL: JERUSALEM

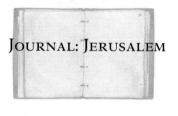

# JOURNAL: JERUSALEM

_____

_____

_____

_____

_____

_____

_____

_____

_____

_____

_____

_____

_____

_____

_____

_____

_____

_____

_____

_____

_____

_____

_____

**Fact Finder:** _There was another gate mentioned when Jeremiah was arrested trying to leave the city to claim his share of property among the people of Benjamin. What was the name of that gate?_ Jeremiah 37:13

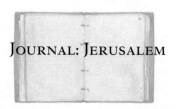

# Journal: Jerusalem

DEAD SEA
MASADA
EIN GEDI
QUMRAN

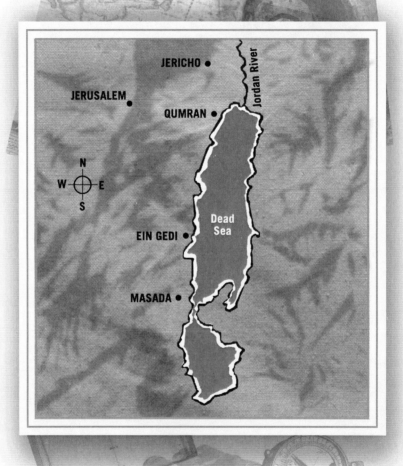

# CHAPTER 9: DEAD SEA

## DEAD SEA

*All these latter kings joined forces in the Valley of Siddim (that is, the Dead Sea Valley).* Genesis 14:3

What we call the "Dead Sea" is actually an inaccurate translation of its Hebrew name, Yam ha Maved, which means the "Killer Sea." Though deadly to most living creatures, the Dead Sea has attracted human visitors from around the Mediterranean basin for thousands of years. David used it as a refuge; Herod used it as a health resort; Egyptians used balm from the Dead Sea for mummification; and even today people use the salts and minerals from the Dead Sea to create cosmetics.

The Dead Sea is the lowest place on earth, at roughly 1,300 feet below sea level. It is about 40 miles long, 11 miles across at its widest point, and 1400 feet deep. At 28-35 percent salt content (or 300 grams of salt per kilogram), it is twice as salty as the Great Salt Lake in Utah and 8.6 times as salty as the ocean. The sea is completely landlocked and the deeper you go the saltier it gets. Why is it so salty? Well, the Dead Sea is so low that it can't drain, and 7 million tons of water evaporates from it every day, leaving behind the minerals that flowed in with the water, including salt.

The surface, fed by the Jordan River, is the least salty. As you go deeper, the water becomes so salty that it literally can't hold any more salt and the salt begins to pile up on the bottom of the sea.

Visitors can float effortlessly on the waters of the Dead Sea because of the extremely high concentration of dissolved mineral salts in the water. Increased density means our bodies are more buoyant in the Dead Sea—so you bob like a cork. In fact, people are so buoyant in this water it makes it tough to actually swim. Most people like to just kick back in the water and read. The dry air, year-round warm temperatures, and therapeutic value of this place makes it quite a tourist destination.

Except for simple organisms, no plant or animal life is found in the Dead Sea. Fish that accidentally swim into the waters from one of the several freshwater streams that feed the sea are killed instantly, their bodies quickly coated with a preserving layer of salt crystals and then tossed onto shore by the wind and waves. And this is no ordinary table salt, either. The salts found in the Dead Sea are mineral salts, just like you find in the oceans.

Jordan River enters the Dead Sea on the left    Cliffs along Dead Sea shoreline
*Photos: Todd Bolen*

In the strange-but-true category, if there is a very rainy winter, the Dead Sea can temporarily come back to life. In 1980, after one such rainy winter, the normally dark blue Dead Sea turned red. Researchers found that the increased amounts of rainwater had lowered the salt content, which in turn allowed a type of red-colored algae to grow. Another weird feature of the Dead Sea is that it regularly spits up asphalt.

Due to its mineral waters, the Dead Sea has a long history as a medicinal spa. Aristotle, the Queen of Sheba, King Solomon, and Cleopatra were all familiar with the benefits of the mineral waters. Still today, health spas and hot springs dot the shoreline of the Dead Sea and doctors advise patients with skin ailments to soak in its waters.

Archaeological ruins are scattered throughout the area. Masada and Qumran are both nearby, but the area is best known as the former site of the biblical towns of Sodom and Gomorrah. South of the sea, on the way to Eilat, is a rock salt formation that tourists are told is Lot's wife. According to the Bible, Lot's wife ignored God's admonition not to look back at the cities He was destroying as they fled, and was turned into a pillar of salt (Genesis 19:26).

## DEAD SEA IN THE BIBLE

The lake was not known as the Dead Sea until the 2nd century AD. The Old Testament refers to it as the Salt Sea (Genesis 14:3; Joshua 3:16), the Sea of Arabah (Deuteronomy 3:17), the Eastern Sea (Ezekiel 47:18; Joel 2:20), and the Sea (Ezekiel 47:1-11).

In ancient times, the Dead Sea was a great natural barrier blocking traffic to Judah from the east. An advancing army of Ammonites and Moabites apparently crossed a shallow part of the Dead Sea on their way to attack King Jehoshaphat (2 Chronicles 20). Sodom and Gomorrah (Genesis 18:20-33) and the three other "Cities of the Plain" (Deuteronomy 29:23) were somewhere on these shores. Before their destruction, the Dead Sea was a green valley, which was called the Vale of Siddim. King David was said to have hidden from Saul at Ein Gedi nearby.[1]

---

According to prophecies in both Ezekiel and Zechariah, one day the Dead Sea will be utterly transformed, allowing this body of water to sustain life again. Take some time to read the following, fascinating passage:

POINTS FROM THE PASTOR

*Then he led me back to the bank of the river. When I arrived there, I saw a great number of trees on each side of the river. He said to me, "This water flows toward the eastern region and goes down into the Arabah, where it enters the Dead Sea. When it empties into the sea, the salty water there becomes fresh. Swarms of living creatures will live wherever the river flows. There will be large numbers of fish, because this water flows there and makes the salt water fresh; so where the river flows everything will live. Fishermen will stand along the shore; from En Gedi to En Eglaim there will be places for spreading nets. The fish will be of many kinds—like the fish of the Mediterranean Sea. But the swamps and marshes will not become fresh; they will be left for salt. Fruit trees of all kinds will grow on both banks of the river. Their leaves will not wither, nor will their fruit fail. Every month they will bear fruit, because the water from the sanctuary flows to them. Their fruit will serve for food and their leaves for healing." * Ezekiel 47:6-12

Here in the heart of Israel, God has once again written a lesson for us in 3D—no goofy glasses necessary. The lesson is so clear that even a child can understand it: What was once polluted and dead will live again when the Living Water flows through it. In John 4:10-13, John 7:38, and Revelation 7:17, we learn that Jesus Christ possesses that Living Water. And as you float in the Dead Sea or sit on its shore, remember that the Lord is the Author of Life, Restorer, and Healer, and there is nothing He can't bring back to life!

## MASADA

Picture the towering mesas of Arizona and you'll have a pretty good idea of what to expect at Masada. Masada means "fortress" and it's not hard to understand how it got its name. The site stands like an island of stone hundreds of feet above the plain surrounding it. With sheer cliff sides that range between 300 and 1300 feet high it's the perfect place to build a fort.

According to Josephus, Herod the Great wanted a safe place to retreat in case of revolt, so he fortified Masada between 37 and 31 BC. During the first Jewish-Roman war (66 AD) it fell into the hands of the Jewish zealots, and after the destruction of the Second Temple (70 AD), the Jewish rebels and their families fled to this mountain-top fortress, using it as a base for raiding Roman settlements.

The natural fortifications, the narrow, winding path to the protected gate, the rainwater cisterns, the storehouses, barracks, and armory (built by Herod), made this place seem indestructible. The zealots knew they couldn't beat Rome; they hoped to wait them out. They were so few—maybe Rome wouldn't consider them worth the cost of a long, drawn-out siege. That hope died in 72 AD when Rome marched against Masada.

At first, the Romans tried to breach the wall. When that failed they came up with a new plan; they would build an earthen ramp on the shortest side. The Romans used Jewish slaves to build the ramp so that the Jews on Masada would not roll rocks down the hill to kill them. By spring of 73 AD, the ramp was complete.

Meanwhile, the Jews on Masada realized that they were going to be conquered and they knew what defeat at the hands of the Romans would cost—slavery for the wives and children and execution for the men. Their leader, Eleazar ben Yair, proposed a drastic solution. Each man would kill his own family and then the men would kill each other. Two women and five children hid in cisterns to avoid being killed. From these survivors and from Josephus who recorded their story, we have Eleazar's final speech to his people:

Aerial view of Masada and Roman siege ramp     "Herod's Pool"    *Photos: Todd Bolen*

"Since we have long ago resolved never to be servants to the Romans, nor to any other than to God Himself, Who alone is the true and just Lord of mankind…it is still in our power to die bravely and in a state of freedom. Let our wives die before they are abused and our children before they have tasted of slavery and after we have slain them, let us bestow that glorious benefit upon each other."

Eleazar also ordered that all Jewish possessions be burned except for the food. Why? He wanted the Romans to know that the zealots hadn't fallen due to weakness. They had chosen their own destiny: death before slavery. By the time the Romans entered the fort the 960 defenders were already dead.

The history of Masada was recorded by Josephus but was pretty much forgotten until 1842, when archaeologist Yigael Yadin began to excavate the site. Then, in the 1920s a Jewish writer named Isaac Lamdan wrote a poem titled "Masada" which retold the story of what happened here. Written more than a decade before the Holocaust the opening lines are eerily prophetic:

> "Who are you that come,
> Stepping in heavy silence?
> The remnant.
> Alone I remained on the great day of slaughter.
> Alone, of father and mother, sisters and brother."

As European Jews began to face Nazi persecution, this history of Jewish resistance in the face of a seemingly unbeatable enemy shone like a light. It inspired Jews to join the resistance and even helped inspire the uprising in the Warsaw Ghetto. This place—where 960 men, women, and children committed suicide—became a symbol of Jewish resistance and survival. Today, after completing basic training, Israeli soldiers climb the Snake Path at night and are sworn in at this site. After taking the oath of allegiance they shout, "Masada shall not fall again!"

## Masada in the Bible

Although Masada is not mentioned in the Bible by name, it is possible that this was David's place of refuge during his flight from Saul and where he wrote some of his Psalms. If so, David was probably referring to Masada as the "stronghold" (1 Samuel 22:4-5; 23:14; 24:22), using it to depict God as his fortress and rock of refuge (Psalm 18:2, 31; 71:3; 144:2).[2]

---

Masada is always one of the highlights of a trip to the Holy Land. More of a historical drama than a biblical drama, it captivates the imagination to hear the story of the Jews resisting the Romans and fleeing to this mountain, then taking their own lives rather than being captured alive. This is another one of those places in which you'll want to stick close to your guide, avoid wandering off, and absorb all the details of one incredible story. And with a stunning view of the Dead Sea, the adventure will take you back in time.

There are two ways to get to the top of Masada: one is by cable car and the other is by walking up the Snake Path. Usually, for the sake of time, most guides will put you on the cable car. But if you're up for a challenge, are in excellent health and can afford the extra 45 minutes, get there early to hike to the pla-

Masada Snake Path     *Photo: Dudley Rutherford*

teau. Bring a bottle of water and your camera, and don't forget to purchase a one-way return ticket on the cable car. Enjoy the view and the difficulty of the climb. Looking back on your trip, this will be a memory of a lifetime—a view that will knock your sandals (or hiking shoes) off—and you'll have the pictures to prove you actually climbed Masada.

## Ein Gedi

*And David went up from there and lived in the strongholds of En Gedi.*
1 Samuel 23:29

The 6,250-acre Ein Gedi (or "En Gedi") is a nature reserve and national park in Israel, located west of the Dead Sea, close to Masada and the caves of Qumran. The oldest ruins found in Ein Gedi are from the Chalcolithic period (4000 BC). The remains of this temple are not far from Ein Gedi Spring.

Josephus, the 1st century Roman-Jewish historian, praised Ein Gedi for its palm trees and balsam. The site is known for its caves, springs, and rich diversity of flora and fauna. Thanks to its location, hot climate, and abundant water, Ein Gedi is truly an oasis. Most of the springs around the Dead Sea are salty, but not here. Ein Gedi's fresh water and farmland made it an ideal place to settle.

These days, hikers and nature lovers come to see the wildlife. On any given day, you might see ibex, hyrax, or, very rarely, a leopard.

## Ein Gedi in the Bible

Ein Gedi is mentioned several times in biblical writings. It is first mentioned as part of the area allotted to the tribe of Judah (Joshua 15:62). David hid from Saul in these caves (1 Samuel 24) and later wrote about it in the Song of Solomon 1:14: *My beloved is to me a cluster of henna blossoms from the vineyards of En Gedi.*

Falls at Ein Gedi                    Young ibex              *Photos: Todd Bolen*

Around 1000 BC, Ein Gedi served as one of the main places of refuge for David as he fled from Saul and lived in the strongholds of En Gedi (1 Samuel 23:29). Ein Gedi means literally "the spring of the kid (goat)," and there is evidence that young ibex have always lived near the springs of Ein Gedi. Once, when David was fleeing from King Saul, the pursuers searched the "Crags of the Ibex" in the vicinity of Ein Gedi. It was in a cave near here that David cut off the corner of Saul's robe (1 Samuel 24:4). [3]

POINTS FROM THE PASTOR

If you have the time, Ein Gedi is a great place to walk back to the waterfall. You'll be refreshed by the beauty of the hike and all of the young people playing in the water. Think of David who, somewhere in the cliffs above, was hiding from King Saul and probably used this water source to sustain him in this region.

# Qumran

*In the wilderness: Beth Arabah, Middin, Sekakah, Nibshan, the City of Salt and En Gedi—six towns and their villages.* Joshua 15:61-62

In 1947, the Dead Sea Scrolls were found near the tiny village of Qumran. The scrolls had been hidden in clay jars for nearly 2,000 years, miraculously preserved by the arid climate. Fragments were found with all of the Old Testament books except for the books of Esther and Nehemiah.

Qumran, just 150 feet west of the Dead Sea, is 1,200 feet below sea level. Difficult-to-reach caves dot the steep cliffs to the west of the settlement. Qumran was home to the Essenes, an extreme sect of the Pharisees. Disapproving of religious practices in Jerusalem, they withdrew to Qumran in the wilderness. They lived a communal life and shared their possessions. They practiced frequent baptism and believed the end of the world was near. Essenes never married, because they wanted to be ritually pure when the Lord returned. Men lived outside in the caves away from the women. The Essenes stored their library of scrolls in these caves for safety. The site of this city has been identified as Khirbet Qumran, or the biblical "City of Salt" (see Joshua 15:62).

Local legend says a shepherd threw a rock into a cave in an attempt to drive out a missing animal. The sound of shattering pottery drew him into the cave, where he found several ancient jars containing scrolls wrapped in linen. The scrolls were first brought to a Bethlehem antiquities dealer who returned them after being told that

Qumran Cave 4          Photo: Dudley Rutherford

they had probably been stolen from a synagogue. Next, the scrolls fell into the hands of Khalil Eskander Shahin, nicknamed Kando, a cobbler and antiques dealer.

A portion of the scrolls made their way to Mar Samuel, archbishop of the Syrian Orthodox Church of Antioch. After examining the scrolls, he offered to buy them. He bought four scrolls: the now famous Isaiah

Scroll, the Community Rule, the Habakkuk Peshar, and the Genesis Apocryphon. Soon, more scrolls surfaced in the antiquities market. Professor Eleazer Sukenik, an Israeli archaeologist and scholar at Hebrew University, bought three: The War Scroll, Thanksgiving Hymns, and another more fragmented Isaiah scroll.

The Bedouins, hoping to cash in on the scrolls, kept the location of the caves secret. Archaeologists continued to hunt for the site until the Arab-Israeli War started in 1948. With a war happening, no large-scale search could be made. Finally, in 1949, a UN observer found Cave 1.

It's strange to imagine, but on July 1, 1954, the Dead Sea Scrolls went up for sale in the classified section of the Wall Street Journal! The ad read as follows: "MISCELLANEOUS FOR SALE. THE FOUR DEAD SEA SCROLLS. Biblical manuscripts dating back to at least 200 BC are for sale. This would be an ideal gift to an educational or religious institution by an individual or group. Box F 206 WALL STREET JOURNAL." After a brief stay in New York's Waldorf-Astoria, the scrolls sold for $250,000.

The first archaeologist to excavate at Qumran was Father Roland de Vaux, of the Ecole Biblique in Jerusalem. De Vaux excavated Cave 1 in 1949, and began excavating the site of Qumran in 1951. Using his archaeological knowledge and some good old-fashioned common sense, he made a map of the site. He excavated a scriptorium complete with writing implements and inkwells, which may be the very tools that were used to transcribe the Dead Sea Scrolls!

For more than 2,000 years, the scrolls sat undisturbed, deep in the caves of the Judean desert. It's likely that no more than 200 people lived here, but this long-forgotten sect in this isolated place impacted the world long after it was gone. We will learn more about the Dead Sea Scrolls, housed in the Israel Museum, in Chapter 10.[4]

**POINTS FROM THE PASTOR**

Driving back to Jerusalem after a long day of traveling, climbing to the top of Masada, floating on the surface of the Dead Sea, or hiking to the falls of Ein Gedi, I guarantee you will be exhausted! Beyond the physical fatigue are the mental and emotional fatigue of seeing so many sites and hearing so many facts, and it can be easy to miss out on the importance of the Dead Sea Scrolls. These critical documents help validate the divine inspiration of the Scriptures and build our trust in the canon and doctrine of the Gospel of Jesus Christ.

The discovery of the ancient scrolls in the Judean Desert is perhaps the most important archaeological discovery of the 20th century. Before that time, we possessed no ancient versions of the Bible, and there were Jewish and Christian scholars who contended that changes were made to the Old Testament either to corroborate the revelation of Jesus as the Son of God or to eradicate any evidence relating to Jesus. Thus, the question arose as to whether the Old Testament text as we know it today is identical to what the ancients would have written or whether there were changes made to it.[5]

However, the startling finding at Qumran should leave no doubt in one's mind about the authenticity of the Scriptures. For example, in a document referred to as the "Testimonia" found in Cave 4, a number of Old Testament passages are brought together that formed the basis for the Jewish people's messianic expectations:

- *"I will raise up for them a prophet like you from among their brothers; I will put my words in his mouth, and he will tell them everything I command him."* Deuteronomy 18:18

- *"I see him, but not now; I behold him, but not near. A star will come out of Jacob; a scepter will rise out of Israel. He will crush the foreheads of Moab, the skulls of all the sons of Sheth."* Numbers 24:17

- *"He teaches your precepts to Jacob and your law to Israel. He offers incense before you and whole burnt offerings on your altar. Bless all his skills, O LORD, and be pleased with the work of his hands. Smite the loins of those who rise up against him; strike his foes till they rise no more."* Deuteronomy 33:10-11

Additionally, there were three individuals in the Old Testament who were referred to as "my anointed ones"—the prophet, priest, and king (see Exodus 29:29; 1 Samuel 16:13, 24:6; 1 Kings 19:16; Psalm 105:15). Each of these men was consecrated to his work by an anointing with oil. The Hebrew word for "anointed" is meshiach, which is where we get the word "Messiah." The awesome truth of the New Testament doctrine of the Messiah is that each of these three offices was fulfilled in the person and work of Jesus Christ of Nazareth! See John 6:14; John 7:40; Acts 3:22; Acts 7:37; compare Psalm 110:4 with Hebrews 7; and study Hebrews 9:24-26; Hebrews 10:11-12; Luke 1:32-33; and Revelation 19:16.

The final manuscript I wish to highlight has been reconstructed from 12 small fragments, comprising less than two columns of writing, but its brief contents predict the birth of a special Child, possibly drawing on Isaiah 9:6-7: *For to us a child is born, to us a son is given, and the government will be on his shoulders. And he will be called Wonderful Counselor, Mighty God, Everlasting Father, Prince of Peace.*[6]

I have shared this passage with Jewish and Christian friends alike, who were absolutely astounded that it is actually in the Old Testament. This wonderful Child was born in Bethlehem of the Virgin Mary, and His name is Jesus. He is the Prophet, Priest, and King of Israel.

As we retire from an action-packed day in the region of the Dead Sea, let us give thanks to God for allowing us to find these important scrolls that confirm the existence and identity of Jesus Christ of Nazareth—God's one and only Son. And let us treasure our Savior and this important validation of His Word, remembering that:

*All Scripture is God-breathed and is useful for teaching, rebuking, correcting and training in righteousness, so that the man of God may be thoroughly equipped for every good work. In the presence of God and of Christ Jesus, who will judge the living and the dead, and in view of his appearing and his kingdom, I give you this charge: Preach the Word; be prepared in season and out of season; correct, rebuke and encourage— with great patience and careful instruction. For the time will come when men will not put up with sound doctrine. Instead, to suit their own desires, they will gather around them a great number of teachers to say what their itching ears want to hear.* 2 Timothy 3:16-4:3

MASADA/EIN GEDI/QUMRAN

*Top:* Aerial view of Masada.

*Middle left:* Palms of Ein Gedi against the Dead Sea.

*Middle right:* Masada bathhouse caldarium.

*Left:* Qumran scriptorium.

*Above Middle:* Qumran mikvah steps.

*Above Right:* Masada bathhouse fresco. *Photos: Todd Bolen*

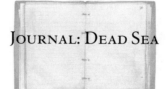

## JOURNAL: DEAD SEA

_____

_____

_____

_____

_____

_____

_____

_____

_____

_____

_____

_____

_____

_____

_____

_____

_____

_____

_____

_____

_____

_____

_____

_____

_____

_____

# JOURNAL: DEAD SEA

_____

_____

_____

_____

_____

_____

_____

_____

_____

_____

_____

_____

_____

_____

_____

_____

_____

_____

_____

_____

_____

_____

_____

_____

_____

_____

_____

The empty tomb                    Photos: Steve Beaumont

PROPHECY
YAD VASHEM
MUSEUMS
GARDEN TOMB
COMMUNION

## CHAPTER 10: FINAL DAY

### A BRIEF LOOK AT PROPHECY

Before we explore Jerusalem's fascinating and state-of-the-art museums and conclude this amazing trip with a visit to the Garden Tomb, let's take a moment to discuss the biblical prophecies concerning the re-gathering of the Jewish people to the Holy Land and the birth, life and death of Jesus Christ. There is no place in the world in which you will gain a greater understanding of these topics than in Israel.

Do you remember when we traveled through Israel's ancient history leading up to her modern history in Chapter 1? We learned how foreign nations continuously invaded and conquered the nation of Israel, and eventually, the Jewish people were exiled and scattered among the nations. However, God made the following promises that He would one day restore His people, re-gathering and reestablishing them as a nation:

*"Who has ever heard of such things?*
*Who has ever seen things like this?*
*Can a country be born in a day*
*or a nation be brought forth in a moment?*
*Yet no sooner is Zion in labor*
*than she gives birth to her children.*
*Do I bring to the moment of birth*
*and not give delivery?" says the LORD.*
*"Do I close up the womb when I bring to delivery?" says your God.*
*"Rejoice with Jerusalem and be glad for her,*
*all you who love her;*
*rejoice greatly with her,*
*all you who mourn over her."* Isaiah 66:8-10

*"See, I will bring them from the land of the north*
*and gather them from the ends of the earth.*
*Among them will be the blind and the lame,*

*expectant mothers and women in labor;*
*a great throng will return.*
*They will come with weeping;*
*they will pray as I bring them back.*
*I will lead them beside streams of water*
*on a level path where they will not stumble,*
*because I am Israel's father,*
*and Ephraim is my firstborn son.*
*Hear the word of the LORD, O nations;*
*proclaim it in distant coastlands:*
*'He who scattered Israel will gather them*
*and will watch over his flock like a shepherd.'"* Jeremiah 31:8-10

*"...and say to them, 'This is what the Sovereign LORD says: I will take the Israelites out of the nations where they have gone. I will gather them from all around and bring them back into their own land. I will make them one nation in the land, on the mountains of Israel. There will be one king over all of them and they will never again be two nations or be divided into two kingdoms. They will no longer defile themselves with their idols and vile images or with any of their offenses, for I will save them from all their sinful backsliding, and I will cleanse them. They will be my people, and I will be their God.'"* Ezekiel 37:21-23

The Israelites had no country for 2,500 years; during that time, I'm sure many naysayers doubted the above prophecies from the Word of God. But then, on May 14, 1948, something miraculous happened. Against all odds and in just a single day, Israel once again became a nation and a people, just as the prophets Jeremiah, Isaiah, and Ezekiel had predicted would happen in the Last Days!

Israel's restoration as a nation is only half of her glorious future—for God promised her a Savior, a Messiah, who ultimately would conquer her enemies and bring peace and eternal rule. The Old Testament contains more than 300 references to the coming Messiah, including 60 distinct prophecies. It was through these prophecies that Israel was told she would be able to recognize the true Messiah when He came. The four Gospels record several times when Jesus said He was fulfilling an Old Testament prophecy. (See Luke 20:17; Luke 24:27; and John 5:46 to name a few.[1]) Entire books have been written and websites have been dedicated to the fulfilled prophecies concerning the birth, life, and death of Jesus. For the sake of time, I will just highlight a few of them; however, I would highly recommend the books New Evidence that Demands a Verdict by Josh MacDowell and The Case for Christ by Lee Strobel.

• The Messiah will be a prophet like Moses, and this was prophesied by Moses himself in Deuteronomy 18:15-19. Like Moses, the Messiah would be a leader, prophet, teacher, lawgiver, deliverer, priest, and a mediator between man and God. He would be one of God's chosen people, a Jew, and would perform many miracles to validate His message. There are many other parallels between the lives of Moses and Jesus; see http://www.christiananswers.net/dictionary/ messianicprophecies.html.

• Genesis chapters 17 and 21 state that the Messiah will be a descendant of Abraham, Isaac, and Jacob. More specifically, He will be a descendant of Judah (Isaiah 11:1-5) and David (2 Samuel 7:12-16; Jeremiah 23:5; Psalm 89:3-4). Jesus fulfilled all of these genealogical requirements; see Matthew 1 and Luke 1:27, 32, 69.

• He will be born in a small city called Bethlehem (Micah 5:2), and this was fulfilled in Luke 2:4-20.

• He will be born of a virgin (Isaiah 7:14), fulfilled in Matthew 1 and Luke 1.

• He will be a priest according to the order of Melchizedek. (Compare Psalm 110:4 with Hebrews 5:6.)

• He will come while the Temple of Jerusalem is still standing (Malachi 3:1; Psalm 118:26; Daniel 9:26; Zechariah 11:13; Haggai 2:7-9). This was fulfilled in Matthew 21:12.

• The Messiah will perform many miracles (Isaiah 35:5-6). See Matthew 9:27-31; 14:25; 15:32-33; 17:24-27; Mark 7:31-37; 8:1-10; 8:22-26; Luke 5:4-11; 7:11-17; 8:41-56; 13:11-17; 14:1-6; 17:11-19; and John 2:1-11; 9:1-7; 11:38-44; 21:1-14—just to name a few of the miracles of Jesus.

• Isaiah 29:18 states that the Messiah will open the eyes of the blind. Jesus fulfilled this prophecy in Matthew 9:27-31; 12:22; 20:29-34; Mark 8:22-26 and 10:46-52; Luke 18:35-43; and John 9:1-7.

• He will speak in parables (Psalm 78:2). Jesus fulfilled this in Matthew 13:34.

• The Gentiles will believe in Him, while His own people will reject Him. Compare Isaiah 8:14; 28:16; 49:6; 50:6; and 60:3 with 1 Peter 2:7.

• A messenger will prepare the way for Him (Isaiah 40:3, Malachi 3:1). John the Baptist fulfilled this prophecy in Matthew 3:1-3, 11:10; John 1:23; and Luke 1:17.

• He will "be cut off, but not for himself" (Daniel 9:26 NKJV), which refers to the crucifixion when Jesus died for the sins of the world.

• The Messiah will enter Jerusalem riding a donkey. See Zechariah 9:9 and its fulfillment in Matthew 21:5 and Luke 19:32-37.

• He will be betrayed by a friend (Psalm 41:9) for the price of 30 pieces of silver (Zechariah 11:12), which was fulfilled in Matthew 26:47-48 and 27:3-5. This money will be used to buy a potter's field (Zechariah 11:13; Matthew 27:6-10).

• He will not open his mouth to defend Himself (Isaiah 53:7 and Matthew 27:12), and He will be beaten and spit upon (Isaiah 50:6 and Matthew 26:67).

• His hands and feet will be pierced (Psalm 22:16 and Zechariah 12:10, fulfilled in Acts 2:23).

• Psalm 34:20 states that the Messiah's bones will not be broken, and this was fulfilled in John 19:33.

• His enemies will divide His clothing and cast lots for them. (See Psalm 22:18 and John 19:23-24.)

• He will not decay, and He will be resurrected from the dead (Psalm 16:10, and fulfilled in Matthew 28:5-6 and Acts 2:31).

• He will ascend into Heaven (Psalm 68:18 and Acts 1:9), and He will be seated at the hand of God (Psalm 110:1 and Hebrews 1:3).

• Finally, Psalm 2:7 states that the Messiah will be the Son of God, and this was fulfilled in Matthew 3:17.

There are many other prophecies that Jesus fulfilled in his birth, life, death, and resurrection, and I encourage you to study these on your own. As you examine these Scriptures and pray and ask God to reveal the truth to you, I am certain that the undeniable proof that Jesus is the Messiah will do more than just knock your sandals off. I pray your heart and life will be changed forever.

Now that we have spent some time considering the prophecies concerning the nation of Israel and the identity of her Messiah, let us move on to our last chapter exploring the Holy Land, starting with a tour of some mesmerizing museums.

## Yad Vashem

Jerusalem's first must-see museum is, without a doubt, Yad Vashem. There is an old saying that goes, "Those who don't learn from history are doomed to repeat it." As the Jewish people's living memorial to the Holocaust, Yad Vashem safeguards the memory of the past and imparts its meaning for future generations. For more than half a century, Yad Vashem has been the world center for documentation, research, education, and commemoration, and is today a dynamic and vital place of intergenerational and international encounter.[2]

Yad Vashem Pillar of Heroism and Memorial to the Deportees          *Photos: Todd Bolen*

Yad Vashem, the Holocaust Martyrs' and Heroes' Remembrance Authority, was established in 1953 by act of the Knesset (Israel's parliament) to memorialize the six million Jewish men, women, and children murdered by the Nazis and their collaborators during the years 1933-1945. Holocaust survivor Abel Herzberg said, "There were not six million Jews murdered; there was one murder, six million times." I think what he meant was that it's impossible to wrap your mind around the death of six million people. Such an astronomical number is difficult both to comprehend and personalize. But when one imagines somebody they love being murdered—then takes the shock, horror, and heartbreak and adds those feelings up one by one until reaching six million—it becomes a lot more personal, doesn't it?

The goal of Yad Vashem is to honor the heroism and courage of the Jewish partisans and the fighters in the Ghetto revolts, as well as the actions of the "Righteous among the Nations" (non-Jews who saved the lives of Jews). Located on Har Hazikaron (Hill of Remembrance), the Yad Vashem Memorial and Institute has several commemorative monuments, a museum, a central archive, and a research center for the documentation of the Holocaust.

One of the most somber memorials at Yad Vashem is the Hall of Remembrance. It is an austere, concrete-walled structure with a low, tent-like roof. It stands empty except for an eternal flame. As you walk inside the building, look down. Carved into the black basalt floor, you'll see the names of 21 Nazi extermination camps, concentration camps, and killing sites in central and Eastern Europe. A crypt in front of the memorial flame contains ashes of victims.

Take a moment as you approach the Hall of Remembrance to notice the trees that line the entrance. They were planted in honor of non-Jewish men and women—the "Righteous among the Nations"—who, at the risk of their own lives, attempted to rescue Jews during the Holocaust. Several of the trees honor Christian clergy, among them a Franciscan priest in Assisi, the bishop of the Greek island of Zakinthos, a Polish nun in Lithuania, and a French Protestant pastor. More than 20,000 individuals have been honored with the title "Righteous among the Nations."

The Valley of the Communities is a 2.5-acre monument that was dug out from the natural bedrock. Engraved on the massive stone walls of the memorial are the names of more than 5,000 Jewish communities that were destroyed, and a few that suffered but survived, in the shadow of the Holocaust.

The Memorial to the Deportees is an original cattle-car, which was used to transport thousands of Jews to the death camps. Perched on the edge of an abyss, it is a gut-wrenching picture of the fate the deportees faced.

In 2005, with about 40 world leaders attending the opening ceremony, a new Holocaust History Museum was unveiled. Replacing the one built in the 1960s, Yad Vashem's Holocaust Museum is an almost 600 foot-long linear structure, mainly underground, in the form of a spike that cuts through the mountain. A skylight pierces through the Mount of Remembrance with galleries or exhibition halls branching off the shaft, each dedicated to a different chapter of the Holocaust. At the end of the museum's historical narrative is the Hall of Names—a repository for the Pages of Testimony of millions of Holocaust victims and a memorial to those who perished. As you exit, take some time to survey the beautiful, panoramic view of Jerusalem from the museum's balcony.

The Yad Vashem Archive is the largest collection on the Holocaust in the world. There are 55 million pages of documents, nearly 100,000 photographs, video, audio, and written testimonies of survivors stored here. A study area is attached in which visitors may perform online searches for Holocaust victims' names on the Central Database. Classes are offered in seven languages and the school regularly sends its staff out to teach about the Holocaust.[3]

POINTS FROM THE PASTOR

However little time one has in Jerusalem, visiting the Yad Vashem memorial is essential. I beg you not to miss this opportunity. I must forewarn you—it forever will change your perspective on the Holocaust and those who suffered unjustly, simply because they were Jewish. Requiring at least a half of a day, this sobering experience will shake you to your core. We must never forget the slaughter of millions of innocent people. Life is to be valued as sacred and holy, and still today the Jewish people—God's chosen ones—around the world are persecuted simply for being Jewish.

It's hard to believe, but the president of Iran has actually called for the complete annihilation of the nation of Israel.[4] In fact, he has questioned whether or not the Holocaust even happened.[5] Yet again, I am reminded of the Word of God in Genesis 12:3, *"I will bless those who bless you, and whoever curses you I will curse; and all peoples on earth will be blessed through you."*

While viewing the different areas of the Yad Vashem, make sure you visit the Children's Memorial. Of the six million Jews who were murdered at the hands of Nazi Germany, 1.5 million of them were innocent children. The Children's Memorial is an underground cavern, a dark and somber space; but when you walk inside, it is as if you are standing in the heavens. You will see memorial candles—a customary Jewish tradition to remember the dead—reflected infinitely in the darkness, creating the impression of millions of stars shining in the firmament. A feat of architectural genius, there is actually only one memorial candle,[6] but its appearance is multiplied innumerably via mirrors within the floor and ceiling. The flickering flames of the memorial candles are a reminder to us that ultimately the light conquers the dark. As you make your way around the circular path, you will hear the roll call of the children's names and their countries of residence. Will you please take a few minutes to say a prayer on behalf of Israel? Ask God to protect and bless them, and recommit your life to do whatever you can possibly do to support the nation of Israel.

## ISRAEL MUSEUM

The Israel Museum, founded in May 1965, is best known for the architecturally unique Shrine of the Book, which houses the Dead Sea Scrolls collection and other rare manuscripts. At first glance, the building looks pretty odd, but it has a story. You will notice right away the white dome, reflected by a pool of water that surrounds it. Across from the white dome is a black basalt wall. The colors and shapes of the building are based on the imagery of the Scroll of the War of the Sons of Light against the Sons of Darkness—a manual for military organization and strategy that was discovered among the Dead Sea Scrolls. The white dome symbolizes the Sons of Light and the black wall symbolizes the Sons of Darkness.

It is said that the above-ground, domelike portion of the building mimics the lids of the jars that once held the Dead Sea Scrolls. Two-thirds of the building is below ground with the treasure inside. So, when you enter the building it's almost as if you're stepping into one of the jars that held and protected these scrolls for 2,000 years.

Israel Museum's Shrine of the Book                    *Photo: Todd Bolen*

An elaborate, seven-year planning process preceded the building's eventual construction in 1965. It was funded by the family of David Samuel Gottesman, a Hungarian émigré and philanthropist who had purchased the scrolls as a gift to the State of Israel.

As mentioned in our Qumran section of Chapter 9, the Dead Sea Scrolls were found between 1947 and 1956, scattered throughout 11 different caves near Khirbet Qumran. One thousand years older than any other known biblical text of the time, the scrolls include every Old Testament book, partially or wholly, except Esther and Nehemiah. The entire book of Isaiah also was found, in addition to 200 copies of Old Testament books.

Keep in mind, these scrolls date from 300 BC to 100 AD and were quite fragmented. To give you an idea of the work that was involved in their reconstruction, take 100 boxes of 1,000-piece puzzles, remove half of the pieces from each box, and dump the remaining pieces into one giant bag. Then, shake up the bag, dump the pieces out, and attempt to reassemble the puzzles. As you can imagine, this had to have been a tedious and meticulous undertaking to say the least!

Once the Dead Sea Scrolls were reconstructed, the fragility of these ancient documents made it impossible to display them all on a continuous basis. Therefore, a system of rotation is used. After a scroll has been exhibited for three to six months, it is removed from its showcase and placed temporarily in a special storeroom, where it "rests" from exposure.

Also on display in the Shrine of the Book are the War Scroll, the Temple Scroll, the Manual of Discipline, and the 10th century Aleppo Codex. The Aleppo Codex was not part of the Dead Sea Scroll find, but it is kept here because it is the oldest complete Bible in Hebrew.

Besides the Shrine of the Book, the Israel Museum has three collection wings: archaeology, Jewish art and life, and the fine arts. The Samuel and Saidye Bronfman Archaeology Wing houses a unique collection of artifacts from the Holy Land and takes visitors through seven "chapters" of a historical narrative that includes Italy, Greece, Egypt, and the Islamic world. The Jack, Joseph, and Morton Mandel Wing for Jewish Art and Life "presents the material culture of Jewish communities worldwide, from the Middle Ages to the present day, and is conceived to provide a view of Jewish life that integrates both its sacred and its secular dimensions."[7] The Edmond and Lily Safra Fine Arts Wing features an extensive and gorgeous collection of European Art, Modern Art, Contemporary Art, Israeli Art, the Arts of Africa, Oceania, and the Americas, Asian Art, Photography, Design and Architecture, and Prints and Drawings.

If you have time, you must explore the Billy Rose Art Garden, located on the western slope of the Museum's campus. Designed by the Japanese-American sculptor Isamu Noguchi, the Art Garden brings together a broad array of cultures such as the Far East, the Near East, and the West, and it features works from late 19th century artists (such as Auguste Rodin, Emile-Antoine Bourdelle, and Aristide Maillol) and renowned 20th artists (such as Pablo Picasso, Alexander Archipenko, Henry Moore, Claes Oldenburg, Richard Serra, and Joel Shapiro). Prominent Israeli artists are also represented, such as Menashe Kadishman, Igael Tumarkin, Ezra Orion, and Benni Efrat.

Remember, the Model City, which we discussed in Chapter 7, is also located here on the campus of the Israel Museum.[8]

## ROCKEFELLER MUSEUM

Situated in a white limestone building in East Jerusalem near Herod's Gate, the Rockefeller Archaeological Museum showcases regional ar-

Rockefeller Museum       *Photo: Todd Bolen*

chaeological finds ranging from the Stone Age to the 18th century. Thousands of these artifacts were unearthed during excavations in Israel (Ottoman Palestine) between the years 1919 and 1948. The museum is named after John D. Rockefeller, who financed its construction with a gift of $2 million in 1927—an enormous amount of money at the time. The museum opened in 1938.

Many of the artifacts were excavated in Acre and Galilee by American and English archaeologists. This extraordinary collection of antiquities is arranged in chronological order and includes a 9,000-year old statue from Jericho, gold jewelry from the Bronze Age, and much more. Pottery, tools, and household effects are arranged by periods: Iron Age, Persian, Hellenistic, Roman, and Byzantine.

Other highlights of the collection are carved wooden panels from the Al-Aqsa Mosque in the 9th century; Crusader stonework that once adorned the entrance to the Church of the Holy Sepulchre; Hellenistic and Roman objects found in the Judean desert caves; and richly ornamented early Islamic architectural details from the 8th century Hisham's Palace near Jericho. There is also a special gallery of Egyptian antiquities, and the bones of Mount Carmel Man are in the south gallery's Paleolithic section. The museum also holds a number of the Dead Sea Scrolls, the bulk of which are in the Israel Museum.[9]

Inside the courtyard of the museum stands one of the most ancient pine trees in the country. According to legend, on the site of this pine tree Ezra the Scribe sat and wrote the Torah for Israel.[10]

## TOWER OF DAVID MUSEUM

Near Jaffa Gate, the historic entrance to the Old City, the Tower of David Museum presents the history of Jerusalem from its beginnings in the 2nd millennium BC until the time it became the capital of the State of Israel in the late 1940s. It also details Jerusalem's significance to Judaism, Christianity, and Islam. The museum is located in the medieval citadel known as the Tower of David, which offers a breathtaking, 360-degree view of the Old City and the modern areas of Jerusalem.

Using diverse, illustrative techniques such as videos, dioramas, and computer graphics—as well as explanations in Hebrew, Arabic, and English—the museum showcases the different periods of the city of Jerusalem in a vivid way. It stages both permanent and temporary exhibitions of history and art, as well as "The Night Spectacular," a unique sound and light show that is the only one of its kind in the world.[11] Also hosted here are lectures and special events in music, dance, drama, and education.

This not-to-be-missed exhibition will deepen your understanding of a city that is unique in the pages of human history, as it presents the main events of the city's history in chronological sequence. The very stones of the citadel's 500-year-old walls are part of Jerusalem's living history.

## GARDEN TOMB

*Later, Joseph of Arimathea asked Pilate for the body of Jesus. Now Joseph was a disciple of Jesus, but secretly because he feared the Jewish leaders. With Pilate's permission, he came and took the body away. He was accompanied by Nicodemus, the man who earlier had visited Jesus at night. Nicodemus brought a mixture of myrrh and aloes, about seventy-five pounds. Taking Jesus' body, the two of them wrapped it, with the spices, in strips of linen. This was in accordance with Jewish burial customs. At the place where Jesus was crucified, there was a garden, and in the garden a new tomb, in which no one had ever been laid. Because it was the Jewish day of Preparation and since the tomb was nearby, they laid Jesus there.* John 19:38-42

The Garden Tomb is the alternative to the Church of the Holy Sepulchre as the actual site of Jesus' burial in Jerusalem. But it wasn't always called the "Garden Tomb." For years it was called "Gordon's Calvary" after the man who discovered it.

One of eleven children, General C.G. Gordon accepted Christ in his early twenties while serving as an army engineer. Ten years later while nursing his dying father, his Christian walk became much more serious; he described it as "throwing aside the religion of the pew."

Gordon was not a man of half measures; from this point on he gave away 90 percent of his salary. He met with William Booth, the founder of the Salvation Army, to strategize ways to help England's poor, and spent his off-duty hours teaching the neediest children in Ragged Schools, which later led to England's first public schools. General Gordon made no attempt to separate his personal faith from his public actions. Instead, his faith formed his actions. When he was made

Entrance to the Garden Tomb today and rock formation nearby          *Photos: Todd Bolen*

Governor General of Sudan, he used his position to stop the slave trade in the region. While serving as the private secretary to the Viceroy of India, he supported the idea of "native rule," which stated that a country was best ruled by its own people.

General Gordon served with distinction and was decorated several times. The newspapers loved this guy. He was the living, breathing embodiment of all that was good about England: faith, duty, and heroism. [12]

In 1883, while between military assignments, he decided to visit the Holy Land. We don't have a written account of Gordon's reaction to the Church of the Holy Sepulchre, but we do have the accounts of others. Mark Twain described it as "...clap-trap side-shows and unseemly impostures of every kind." Herman Melville said of the site, "All is glitter and nothing is gold. A sickening cheat." These responses were likely due to the fact that the Church of the Holy Sepulchre was shared by no less than six denominations during this period. As discussed previously, this made for frequent and ugly clashes, leaving many evangelical Protestants shocked and disappointed by what they saw. This was the Church of the Holy Sepulchre that Gordon would have seen.

While in Palestine, the English general heard about a German theologian, Otto Thenius, who had proposed a different site for Christ's burial in the 1840s. Gordon decided to investigate. He found a site that was near Calvary with a rock formation that looked very much like a skull (Matthew 27:33; Mark 15:22; Luke 23:33; John 19:17), and he found a tomb. In his book, *Reflections in Palestine*, he proposed that this was the real tomb where Christ had been laid.

Those who favor this site give the following evidence:

- It is outside the city walls (Hebrews 13:12).

- It is next to a large rock that looks like a skull.

- Other tombs have been found nearby.

- One particular tomb has a stone groove, which would have been used as a sort of track to move a large stone over the entrance.

- This site is on what would have been a main road. (The Romans would have wanted a crowd.)

- There is room here for both Peter and John to have entered the tomb and later, for the two angels who spoke to Mary Magdalene (John 20).

We may never be able to say with absolute certainty where Christ was buried. Ultimately, it doesn't really matter; it was only temporary housing anyway. What matters is that He walked out of the tomb, conquering death and making a way for us to be saved. Several times in the Gospels, we see that Jesus went away to a quiet place to pray. Let's follow His example and use our last day to come away and spend time in worship and prayer.[13]

POINTS FROM THE PASTOR

Each and every time I visit the Holy Land, there is one place that remains my favorite part of the tour. That place, without a doubt, is the Garden Tomb. As stated above, there is much discussion on whether or not this is the exact tomb and the exact garden where Jesus was buried and resurrected. In my spirit there is something that resonates within me, and I feel that this was the place. I'm drawn to an experience that stirs my soul like no other, as my heart and soul race back in time when Jesus lay in a tomb with a large stone sealing the entrance.

The first time I ever walked into the Garden Tomb, I literally cried for an hour non-stop. I couldn't control my emotions when I reflected upon what the Lord did for me, how much He loved me, and what it must have been like to be there on that day they laid Jesus inside the Garden Tomb.

Inside this tomb was the dead body of the Messiah, the Lord Jesus Christ. Just three days earlier, He hung upon a rough Roman cross where He shed his crimson blood for the sins of the world and cried, "It is finished." In that moment, salvation was made available to all who believe. (I cry again as I write this portion of the book; it moves me every time.)

For the three days that Jesus was in the tomb, it appears as though the devil had won—that perhaps Jesus was not the Son of the Living God who would rise again on the third day as He had predicted (John 2:18-22). To keep the disciples from removing the dead body of Jesus, the Romans posted a seal at the Garden Tomb (Matthew 27:66), thus ensuring Jesus would remain inside and that no false rumors would spread about Him conquering the grave.

And then it happened...

On the third day, a day like no other, God breathed life back into the lifeless body of our Lord. The Bible describes it as follows:

*After the Sabbath, at dawn on the first day of the week, Mary Magdalene and the other Mary went to look at the tomb. There was a violent earthquake, for an angel of the Lord came down from heaven and, going to the tomb, rolled back the stone and sat on it. His appearance was like lightning, and his clothes were white as snow. The guards were so afraid of him that they shook and became like dead men. The angel said to the women, "Do not be afraid, for I know that you are looking for Jesus, who was crucified. He is not here; he has risen, just as he said. Come and see the place where he lay. Then go quickly and tell his disciples: 'He has risen from the dead and is going ahead of you into Galilee. There you will see him.' Now I have told you." So the women hurried away from the tomb, afraid yet filled with joy, and ran to tell his disciples.* Matthew 28:1-8

Reading about this story is one thing, but walking inside the empty tomb and seeing for ourselves that Jesus has risen from the dead changes everything. Romans 10:9-10 states, *That if you confess with your mouth, "Jesus is Lord," and believe in your heart that God raised him from the dead, you will be saved. For it is with your heart that you believe and are justified, and it is with your mouth that you confess and are saved.*

If you came on this trip with any doubts that Jesus Christ is Lord and Savior, it is my prayer that all your uncertainty will be forever removed because of what you have read, seen, and experienced here in Israel. And if you still need more evidence, prayerfully consider the astonishing, fulfilled, biblical prophecies that are listed at the beginning of this chapter concerning the re-gathering of the Jews to the Holy Land as well as Christ's birth, life, death, and resurrection.

Why not take a few moments to journal your thoughts and feelings about what you've seen and what you believe?

_____

_____

_____

_____

_____

_____

_____

_____

_____

_____

_____

_____

Also, take some time to read these verses, and then I want you to write out in your own words what each passage is telling you:

*For all have sinned and fall short of the glory of God...* Romans 3:23

_____

_____

_____

_____

_____

*For the wages of sin is death, but the gift of God is eternal life in Christ Jesus our Lord.* Romans 6:23

_____

_____

_____

_____

_____

*But God demonstrates His own love for us in this: While we were still sinners, Christ died for us.* Romans 5:8

_____

_____

_____

_____

_____

*If you declare with your mouth, "Jesus is Lord," and believe in your heart that God raised him from the dead, you will be saved. For it is with your heart that you believe and are justified, and it is with your mouth that you profess your faith and are saved.* Romans 10:9-10

_____

_____

_____

_____

_____

*Or don't you know that all of us who were baptized into Christ Jesus were baptized into his death? We were therefore buried with him through baptism into death in order that, just as Christ was raised from the dead through the glory of the Father, we too may live a new life. For if we have been united with him in a death like his, we will certainly also be united with him in a resurrection like his.* Romans 6:3-5

---

_____

_____

_____

_____

---

## COMMUNION AT THE GARDEN TOMB

Our word communion comes from the Greek word koinonia (coy-nohn-ee-ah). The word occurs many times in the Bible and no English word can fully express it. Our closest translations are words like community, sharing, intimacy, fellowship, joint participation, and alliance, but they do not capture the depth of this word's meaning entirely. In Greek literature, the word is used to describe marriage—both the living together and the sharing of all things. It is also used to describe business relationships when you "have a share" in something. It is never passive (being together), but is always active (doing together).

Communion (koinonia) is more than the breaking of the bread; it is a collective declaration that "We are one body." A powerful example of what koinonia should look like can be found in a study of the phrase "one another" in the Bible. Scripture commands us to be devoted to one another (Romans 12:10), honor one another (Romans 12:10), live in harmony with one another (Romans 12:16; 1 Peter 3:8), accept one another (Romans 15:7), serve one another in love (Galatians 5:13), be kind and compassionate to one another (Ephesians 4:32), admonish one another (Colossians 3:16), encourage one another (1 Thessalonians 5:11; Hebrews 3:13), spur one another on toward love and good deeds (Hebrews 10:24), offer hospitality (1 Peter 4:9), and love one another (1 Peter 1:22; 1 John 3:11; 3:23; 4:7; 4:11-12). That is what true biblical koinonia should look like.

Most of us are aware of the Communion that was shared between Christ and His disciples at the Last Supper in Matthew 26, Mark 14, and Luke 22. But to help us to embrace the meaning of Communion even further, let us consider the Communion that took place after Christ resurrected from the dead.

The first to see the risen Christ was Mary Magdalene, but the disciples did not believe her report (Mark 16:9-11). The second to see the risen Christ were the two unidentified travelers on the road to Emmaus (Luke 24). Keep in mind that they'd already walked seven miles with Jesus at this point in the story. If they were walking at an average pace, that means they had spent a little more than two hours with Him on the road, but they didn't recognize Him until He broke bread with them. The picture here is that, at some level, Communion reveals Christ to us.

*"When he was at the table with them, he took bread and blessed it, and breaking it, He began giving it to them. Then their eyes were opened and they recognized Him..."* Luke 24:30-31

---

It is only fitting that we conclude our trip with a time of Communion. Jesus knew there was a chance that one day we would forget exactly what He did for us when He died upon the cross. Therefore, He instituted what is called "the Lord's Supper," or "Communion." Shortly before He walked down the Via Dolorosa, He gathered His disciples in the upper room and lovingly commanded them to be ever faithful in taking this sacred supper and to always, *"Do this in remembrance of me."* (See Luke 22:17-20; Acts 20:7; and 1 Corinthians 11:24-26.)

What imagery for our senses—to hold in our hands the bread and the juice, and to understand that it represents Christ's body that was sacrificed and his blood that was shed on behalf of our sins. Communion declares our unity, reveals Christ, proclaims His death, causes us to examine ourselves, and reminds us of His victory. With this in mind, I cannot think of any better way to end our time here in the Holy Land than by taking Communion.

*For whenever you eat this bread and drink this cup, you proclaim the Lord's death until he comes. So then, whoever eats the bread or drinks the cup of the Lord in an unworthy manner will be guilty of sinning against the body and blood of the Lord. Everyone ought to examine themselves before they eat of the bread and drink from the cup.* 1 Corinthians 11:26-28

Aerial view of Jerusalem (Dome of the Rock and Old City is center left)     *Photo: Todd Bolen*

## Saying Goodbye, But Never Forgetting

This brings us to the end of our tour, but hopefully the beginning of a life forever changed as we've experienced together the reality of the death, burial, and resurrection of Jesus Christ. I pray that this journey through the Holy Land has enriched and strengthened your faith. The pages of the Bible have been contested throughout history, and it is often the discoveries made in Israel that refute these challenges and corroborate the truth of God's Word. Every time you read Genesis to Revelation, may each sentence come alive like never before. And whenever you hearken back to the unforgettable sights, sounds, smells, feelings, and emotions you've experienced here in the Holy Land— and the biblical evidence you've seen firsthand—may it never ever cease to knock your sandals off![14]

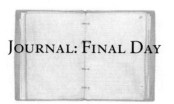

# JOURNAL: FINAL DAY

_____

_____

_____

_____

_____

_____

_____

_____

_____

_____

_____

_____

_____

_____

_____

_____

_____

_____

_____

_____

_____

_____

_____

_____

JOURNAL: FINAL DAY

_____

_____

_____

_____

_____

_____

_____

_____

_____

_____

_____

_____

_____

_____

_____

_____

_____

_____

_____

_____

_____

_____

_____

_____

_____

_____

_____

_____

_____

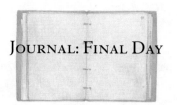

# JOURNAL: FINAL DAY

# FOOTNOTES

Please note: The information provided in this book is meant to be a general background outlining Israel's history and biblical locations—many of which were discovered centuries after lying in ruin. Some dates have been estimated by the experts and oftentimes contrasting information is cited when looking for the facts. If there are any perceived errors in this book, we sincerely apologize and understand that we could have based our information on source material that is in error. We do know that the Bible, which we also used in the research for this book, is perfect and true (2 Timothy 3:16-17).

Foreword From Pastor Dudley
1. Pilgrim's Progress: A Spiritual Guide for the Holy Land Traveler. Robert and Gwynneth Wallace. 1997 The United States Church Publishing House, Canada.

*Chapter 1* Travel to Israel
1. http://en.wikipedia.org/wiki/Maccabees
2. http://en.wikipedia.org/wiki/Zionist_Movement
3. http://eng.mni.gov.il/FinanceIsrael/Pages/En/News/201001.aspx
4. Many facts on Israel were also found on the following websites:
   http://www.jewishvirtuallibrary.org/jsource/History/jerbible.html
   http://en.wikipedia.org/wiki/Israel#Independence_and_first_years
   http://www.keyway.ca/htm2003/20030910.htm

*Chapter 2* Mediterranean Coast
1. http://en.wikipedia.org/wiki/Tel_Aviv
2. http://en.wikipedia.org/wiki/Global_city
3. http://www.lboro.ac.uk/gawc/rb/rb57.html
4. http://www.euromonitor.com/euromonitor-internationals-top-city-destinations-ranking/article
5. http://www.visit-tlv.com/
6. http://www.digitalpodcast.com/detail-Israel_Old_Jaffa_Tour-19088.html

7.  Many facts on the Mediterranean Coast were also found on the
    following websites:
    http://en.wikipedia.org/wiki/Mediterranean_Sea
    http://www.keyway.ca/htm2002/mediter.htm
    http://www.jewishvirtuallibrary.org/jsource/vie/Netanya.html
    http://en.wikipedia.org/wiki/Netanya,_Israel
8.  Haberfeld, Fodor's Israel, p. 200
9.  Jesus and His World, p. 33
10. Flavius Josephus, War II 9.2
11. Pilgrim's Progress (1997 version) by Robert and Gwynneth Wallace
12. Haberfeld, Fodor's Israel, p. 200
13. Flavius Josephus, Jewish Antiquities 19.343-350
14. Many facts on Caesarea were also found on the following websites:
    http://www.padfield.com/1996/caesmari.html
    http://www.keyway.ca/htm2003/20030428.htm
    http://www.pbs.org/wgbh/pages/frontline/shows/religion/maps/arch/
        caesarea.html
    http://en.wikipedia.org/wiki/Caesarea
    http://www.ancientsandals.com/overviews/caesarea.htm
    http://www.bibleplaces.com/caesarea.htm
15. Many facts on Mt Carmel were also found on the following websites:
    http://www.keyway.ca/htm2003/20030428.htm
    http://en.wikipedia.org/wiki/Mount_Carmel
    http://www.bibleplaces.com/mtcarmel.htm
    http://www.jewishvirtuallibrary.org/jsource/Society_&_Culture/kibbutz.htm
    http://www.padfield.com/2000/elijah.html


*Chapter 3:* Jezreel Valley / Lower Galilee

1.  Many facts on Jezreel Valley were also found on the following websites:
    http://www.jewishvirtuallibrary.org/jsource/Society_&_Culture/geo/Jezreel.
        html
    http://www.bibleplaces.com/jezreelvalley.htm
    http://www.ancientsandals.com/overviews/jezreel.htm
2.  http://www.christiananswers.net/q-abr/abr-a017.html
3.  Many facts on Megiddo were also found on the following websites:
    http://www.jewishvirtuallibrary.org/jsource/Archaeology/Megiddo.html
    http://www.ancientsandals.com/overviews/jezreel.htm
    http://en.wikipedia.org/wiki/Tel_Megiddo

4.  Many facts on Mount Tabor were also found on the following websites:
    http://en.wikipedia.org/wiki/Mount_Tabor
    http://www.bibleplaces.com/mounttabor.htm
    http://www.ancientsandals.com/overviews/mount_tabor.htm
5.  Many facts on Cana were also found on the following website:
    http://www.keyway.ca/htm2000/20000518.htm
6.  Many facts on Nazareth were also found on the following websites:
    http://www.keyway.ca/htm2002/nazareth.htm
    http://www.padfield.com/2002/nazareth.html
    http://www.bibleplaces.com/nazareth.htm
    http://www.ancientsandals.com/overviews/nazareth.htm
7.  Many facts on Sepphoris were also found on the following websites:
    http://www.padfield.com/2004/sepphrois.html
    http://www.bibleplaces.com/sepphoris.htm
    http://www.ancientsandals.com/overviews/sepphoris.htm

*Chapter 4:* Galilee
1.  http://www.ultimatebiblereferencelibrary.com/BibleLands.html
2.  Facts on the Sea of Galilee were also found on the following websites:
    http://www.keyway.ca/htm2002/galilee.htm
    http://en.wikipedia.org/wiki/Sea_of_Galilee
    http://www.bibleplaces.com/seagalilee.htm
    http://www.keyway.ca/htm2002/seagal.htm
    http://www.jewishvirtuallibrary.org/jsource/Society_&_Culture/geo/
        Galilee.html
3.  Many facts on Capernaum were also found on the following websites:
    http://en.wikipedia.org/wiki/Capernaum
    http://www.padfield.com/1998/capern.html
    http://www.keyway.ca/htm2002/capernam.htm
4.  http://www.faulkner.edu/admin/websites/rtrull/rt_courses/life_christ_
        course/teaching%20sections/Sec09overviewloc.htm
5.  Many facts on the Beatitudes were also found on the following websites:
    http://www.keyway.ca/htm2005/20050302.htm
    http://www.bibleplaces.com/mtbeatitudes.htm
6.  Many facts on Tabgha were also found on the following websites:
    http://www.bibleplaces.com/tabgha.htm
    http://www.jewishvirtuallibrary.org/jsource/Archaeology/Tabgha.html
7.  http://en.wikipedia.org/wiki/The_Sea_of_Galilee_Boat

*Chapter 5:* Tiberias

1.   Many facts on Tiberias were also found on the following websites:
     http://www.jewishvirtuallibrary.org/jsource/vie/Tiberias.html
     http://en.wikipedia.org/wiki/Tiberias
     http://www.ancientsandals.com/overviews/tabgha.htm

2.   Many facts on Korazim were also found on the following websites:
     http://en.wikipedia.org/wiki/Chorazin
     http://www.nd.edu/~daune/near_east_arch/chorazin/chorazin.htm
     http://www.churchisraelforum.com/the_cursed_city_of_chorazin.htm

3.   Many facts on Magdala were also found on the following websites:
     http://en.wikipedia.org/wiki/Magdala
     http://www.ancientsandals.com/overviews/migdal.htm
     http://www.keyway.ca/htm2002/marymagd.htm

4.   Many on Caesarea Philippi were also found on the following websites:
     http://www.padfield.com/1996/caesphil.html
     http://www.bibleplaces.com/banias.htm
     http://en.wikipedia.org/wiki/Caesarea_Philippi
     http://www.jewishvirtuallibrary.org/jsource/Society_&_Culture/geo/Philippi.html
     http://www.keyway.ca/htm2000/20000831.htm

*Chapter 6:* Jordan River Valley

1.   Many facts on Jordan River Valley were also found on the following websites:
     http://www.keyway.ca/htm2000/20000406.htm
     http://www.ancientsandals.com/overviews/jordan_river.htm
     http://en.wikipedia.org/wiki/Jordan_River
     http://www.jewishvirtuallibrary.org/jsource/Society_&_Culture/geo/jordan
     river.html

2.   Many facts on Beth She'an were also found on the following websites:
     http://www.rehov.org/project/index.htm
     http://www.jewishvirtuallibrary.org/jsource/vie/Betshean.html
     http://www.bibleplaces.com/bethshean.htm
     http://www.ancientsandals.com/overviews/beth-shan.htm
     http://en.wikipedia.org/wiki/Beit_She'an
     http://www.keyway.ca/htm2006/20061023.htm

3.   http://books.google.com/books?id=3SapTk5iGDkC&pg=PA202&l pg=PA202
     &dq=jericho+825+feet+below&source=bl&ots=8r0H7-O95r&sig=K4F
     ROwOa9b7Af6J_8CNLpbVuJw8&hl=en&ei=2AYhTbrkKo64sAOw5

4.   http://www.historylearningsite.co.uk/Saladin.htm

5.  Many facts on Jericho were also found on the following websites:
    http://en.wikipedia.org/wiki/Jericho
    http://www.jewishvirtuallibrary.org/jsource/vie/Jericho.html
    http://www.bibleplaces.com/jericho.htm
    http://www.keyway.ca/htm2002/jericho.htm
    http://www.padfield.com/2000/jericho.html
6.  http://www.goisrael.com/Tourism_Eng/Tourist+Information/
    Discover+Israel/Cities/Jerusalem.htm
7.  Pilgrim's Progress, the 1997 version, page 66.
8.  http://www.goisrael.com/Tourism_Eng/Tourist+Information/
    Discover+Israel/Cities/Jerusalem.htm

*Chapter 7:* Mount of Olives

1.  http://www.mfa.gov.il/MFA/Facts%20About%20Israel/State/Models%20
    of%20Jerusalem
2.  Many facts on Mount of Olives were also found on the following websites:
    http://www.keyway.ca/htm2006/20061023.htm
    http://en.wikipedia.org/wiki/Mount_of_Olives
    http://www.padfield.com/2001/gethsemane.html
    http://www.jewishvirtuallibrary.org/jsource/vie/Jerusalem3.html
3.  Many facts on the Golden Gate were also found on the following websites:
    http://en.wikipedia.org/wiki/Golden_Gate_(Jerusalem)
    http://www.bible-history.com/jewishtemple/JEWISH_TEMPLEThe_Gold
    en_Gate.htm
    http://focusonjerusalem.com/easterngateinprophecy.html
4.  Many facts on the Kidron Valley were also found on the following websites:
    http://www.christusrex.org/www1/jvc/TVCstat01.html
    http://www.keyway.ca/htm2001/20010322.htm
5.  Many facts on Absalom were also found on the following websites:
    http://www.bible-history.com/sketches/ancient/tomb-absalom.html
    http://www.jewishvirtuallibrary.org/jsource/judaica/
    ejud_0002_0020_0_19939.html

*Chapter 8:* Jerusalem

1.  Many facts on the Old City were also found on the following websites:
    http://www.jewishvirtuallibrary.org/jsource/vie/Jerusalem2.html
    http://en.wikipedia.org/wiki/Old_City_of_Jerusalem
    http://www.goisrael.com/Tourism_Eng/Articles/Attractions/OldCityJerusa
    lem.htm

2.  Many facts on the Old City Gates were also found on the following websites:
    http://www.keyway.ca/htm2003/20030615.htm
    http://en.wikipedia.org/wiki/Old_City_(Jerusalem)
    http://www.bibleplaces.com/oldcitygates.htm
    http://www.jewishvirtuallibrary.org/jsource/vie/Jerusalem2.html

3.  Reprinted with permission from Victor Knowles, founder of Peace on Earth Ministries and author of the Knowlesletter – April 2008, Vol. 16 No. 4.
    http:// www.poeministries.org/Knowlesletter.html

4.  Facts on the Old City Quarters were also found on the following websites:
    http://en.wikipedia.org/wiki/Old_City_of_Jerusalem
    http://www.jewishvirtuallibrary.org/jsource/vie/Jerusalem2.html

5.  http://books.google.com/books?id=g0QQtlJSyOEC&pg=PA959&lp
    g=PA959&dq=is+wailing+wall+a+derogatory+term&source=bl&o
    ts=SLwMZ_2aOS&sig=TQuMFg9J4X0Pd2xK2sf1qW7P6VU&hl=e
    n&ei=7T-nTae1Moi8sQOwi5n5DA&sa=X&oi=book_result&ct=result
    &resnum=7&ved=0CEIQ6AEwBg#v=onepage&q=is%20wailing%20
    wall%20a%20derogatory%20term&f=false

6.  Many facts on the Western Wall were also found on the following websites:
    http://www.bibleplaces.com/westernwall.htm
    http://en.wikipedia.org/wiki/Western_Wall
    http://www.jewishvirtuallibrary.org/jsource/Judaism/Western_Wall.html

7.  http://en.wikipedia.org/wiki/Western_Wall_Tunnel

8.  Many facts on the Rabbi's Tunnel were also found on the following website:
    http://en.wikipedia.org/wiki/Western_Wall_Tunnel

9.  http://en.wikipedia.org/wiki/Hezekiah's_Tunnel

10. Reprinted with permission from Dr. John DeLancey, author of Devotional Treasures from the Holy Land, 2011, CrossHouse Publishing, Garland, TX. Pages 139-140.

11. http://en.wikipedia.org/wiki/Midrash

12. http://www.communityofhopeinc.org/Prayer%20Pages/Saints/james%20lesser. html

13. Many facts on the Temple Mount were also found on the following websites:
    http://www.bibleplaces.com/templemount.htm
    http://en.wikipedia.org/wiki/Temple_Mount
    http://focusonjerusalem.com/historyoftemplemount.html

14. http://en.wikipedia.org/wiki/Foundation_Stone#Role_in_the_Temple

15. Pilgrim's Progress: A Spiritual Guide for the Holy Land Traveler. Robert and Gwynneth Wallace. 1997 The United States Church Publishing House, Canada.

16. Facts on the Dome of the Rock were also found on the following websites:
    http://www.bibleplaces.com/domeofrock.htm
    http://en.wikipedia.org/wiki/Dome_of_the_Rock
17. Many facts on the Al-Aqsa mosque were also found on the following websites:
    http://www.bibleplaces.com/domeofrock.htm
    http://en.wikipedia.org/wiki/Al-Aqsa_Mosque
18. Many facts on St. Anne's Church were also found on the following websites:
    http://www.sacred-destinations.com/israel/jerusalem-st-anne-church.htm
    http://www.christusrex.org/www2/baram/B-st-anne.html
19. Facts on the Pool of Bethesda were also found on the following websites:
    http://en.wikipedia.org/wiki/Pool_of_Bethesda
    http://www.bible-history.com/sketches/ancient/pool-bethesda.html
20. Many facts on the Church of the Holy Sepulchre were also found on the
    following websites:
    http://www.sacred-destinations.com/israel/jerusalem-church-of-holy-
        sepulchre.htm
21. http://www.sacred-destinations.com/israel/jerusalem-church-of-holy-
        sepulchre#2
22. Many facts on Via Dolorosa were also found on the following website:
    http://en.wikipedia.org/wiki/Via_Dolorosa

*Chapter 9:* Dead Sea

1. Many facts on the Dead Sea were also found on the following websites:
   http://en.wikipedia.org/wiki/Dead_Sea
   http://www.jewishvirtuallibrary.org/jsource/vie/Deadsea.html
   http://www.extremescience.com/DeadSea.htm
   http://www.bibleplaces.com/deadsea.htm
   http://www.ancientsandals.com/overviews/dead_sea.htm
2. Many facts on Masada were also found on the following websites:
   http://en.wikipedia.org/wiki/Masada
   http://www.ancientsandals.com/overviews/masada.htm
3. Many facts on Ein Gedi were also found on the following websites:
   http://en.wikipedia.org/wiki/Ein_Gedi
   http://www.bibleplaces.com/engedi.htm
   http://www.parks.org.il/ParksENG/company_card.php3?CNumber=853330
4. Many facts on Qumran were also found on the following websites:
   http://en.wikipedia.org/wiki/Qumran
   http://www.ancientsandals.com/overviews/qumran.htm

http://www.parks.org.il/ParksENG/company_card.php3?CNumber=854515

5.    http://www.antiquities.org.il/article_Item_eng.asp?sec_id=36&subj_
        id=69&id=129&module_id=

6.    http://www.christiananswers.net/q-abr/abr-a023.html

*Chapter 10:* Final Day

1.    http://www.christiananswers.net/dictionary/messianicprophecies.html.

2.    http://www1.yadvashem.org/yv/en/about/index.asp

3.    Many facts on Yad Vashem were also found on the following websites:
        http://www.jewishvirtuallibrary.org/jsource/Holocaust/Vashem.html

4.    http://www.nytimes.com/2005/10/26/world/africa/26iht-iran.html

5.    http://news.bbc.co.uk/2/hi/middle_east/4527142.stm

6.    http://www.msafdie.com/#/projects/yadvashemchildrensholocaustmemorial

7.    http://www.english.imjnet.org.il/htmls/page_1364.aspx?c0=14794&bsp=749

8.    Facts on the Israel Museum were also found on the following websites:
        http://www.sacred-destinations.com/israel/jerusalem-israel-museum.htm

9.    http://www.sacred-destinations.com/israel/jerusalem-rockefeller-archaeologi
        cal-museum.htm

10.   http://en.wikipedia.org/wiki/Rockefeller_Museum

11.   http://www.towerofdavid.org.il/English/The_Museum/About_the_Museum.

12.   http://www.victorianweb.org/history/empire/gordon/mersh2.html

13.   Many facts on the Garden Tomb were also found on the following websites:
        http://www.sacred-destinations.com/israel/jerusalem-garden-tomb.htm
        http://en.wikipedia.org/wiki/Garden_Tomb
        http://www.keyway.ca/htm2002/gardntom.htm

14.   http://www.gotquestions.org

Additionally, the author would like to acknowledge and thank the following authors who generously gave permission to use their words and research throughout this book: Todd Bolen (www.bibleplaces.com), David Padfield (www.padfield.com), and Dr. Terry Hulbert (www.ancientsandals.com).

Answers to FACT FINDERS:

Page 33: 175 years

Page 46: Joppa

Page 54: Spirits of Demons

Page 56: Simon Peter,

        Thomas (called Didymus),

        Nathanael

Page 63: Water into wine

Page 76: (d) Capernaum

Page 94: Healed Centurion's servant

Page 102: Seven demons

Page 110: David

Page 125: Gilgal

Page 134: Jericho

Page 143: Many

Page 150: Holy

Page 198: Benjamin Gate

# ISRAEL FACTS

## The Weather

Look around much of Israel and it will look and feel like you're in Southern California. The weather is generally the same but with more humidity in the summer.

*December/January/February:*
Winter in Israel means temperatures of between 41 to 65 degrees fahrenheit (5-18 degrees centigrade) in Tel Aviv. It may get colder around the Jerusalem mountains to a level of 34 degrees fahrenheit (0 degrees centigrade) at night. Yes it can snow in Jerusalem.

*March/April/May:*
Spring is the nicest season of the year with very comfortable weather. Temperature in Tel Aviv is usually between 61 to 75 degrees fahrenheit (16 to 24 degrees centigrade). Jerusalem is approx. 5.5 degrees fahrenheit cooler because of its elevation.

*June/July/August (and sometimes September):*
Summer is hot in Israel! Israelis usually speak of the heat in terms of temperature + humidity, not just temperature. Temperature in Tel Aviv is usually between 75 to 95 degrees fahrenheit (24 to 35 degrees centigrade). Jerusalem is generally 5.5 degrees fahrenheit cooler. In August, the temperature in Tel Aviv may rise to 108 degrees fahrenheit (42 degrees centigrade) and be mixed with 95% humidity. In Jerusalem those days are as hot, but without the humidity.

*September/October/November:*
Some will argue and say that Autumn is the nicest season of the year in Israel. Temperature in Tel Aviv is usually between 61 to 75 degrees fahrenheit (16 to 24 degrees centigrade). Jerusalem is approx. 5.5 degrees fahrenheit cooler.

# ISRAEL FACTS

## CURRENCY EXCHANGE RATE

Israel's currency is counted in shekels. Like anywhere the exchange rate fluctuates up and down as global market conditions change but hopefully this chart will give you a general guideline on what to expect to pay. (This currency exchange rate was calculated in February of 2012):

1 shekel = .2691 U.S. dollars

1 dollar = 3.7156 shekels
2 dollars = 7.4312 shekels
10 dollars = 37.1559 shekels
20 dollars = 74.3119 shekels
50 dollars = 185.7797 shekels
100 dollars = 371.5594 shekels
1,000 dollars = 3,715.593 shekels

## TIME ZONE DIFFERENCE

**Los Angeles**
**5:00pm Wed**

**Israel**
**3:00am Thurs**

Time zones vary during the year as not every country switches to daylight savings time at the same time. But generally, here's the time difference while you're in Israel:

Los Angeles = 10 hours earlier
Chicago = 8 hours earlier
New York = 7 hours earlier

# PASTOR DUDLEY RUTHERFORD

Dudley Rutherford is the senior pastor of the 10,000-member Shepherd of the Hills Church, which the mayor of Los Angeles has called "the most racially diverse church in Los Angeles." He was the president of the 2011 North American Christian Convention and had the honor of speaking at the memorial service for UCLA legend John Wooden in 2010.

Dudley Rutherford

Dudley has filled in as host for the Frank Pastore show on KKLA-FM, the most listened to Christian talk radio station in the United States. He has had the distinction of speaking for several professional sports teams and has been a featured chapel speaker for the World Series.

In 1987, Dudley moved from the Midwest to California, to become the pastor of Hillcrest Christian Church in northern Los Angeles. Under his leadership, the church grew from 350 to 1,000 people. In 1995, Hillcrest merged with Shepherd of the Hills and became the present-day Shepherd of the Hills Church. Since then, the church has grown to about 10,000 people in attendance within 20 different worship services each weekend throughout the Los Angeles area, including four daughter churches and four satellite campuses.

Dudley earned his bachelor's degree from Ozark Christian College and his master's degree in Church Growth from Hope International University. He also obtained an honorary Doctorate of Divinity from St. Charles University.

Dudley and his wife, Renee, and their three children reside in Porter Ranch (Los Angeles), CA. His other published works are *Unleashed: The Church Turning the World Upside Down*, *Proverbs in a Haystack*, *Romancing Royalty*, *Keeping a Smile on Your Faith*, and *God Has an App for That*.

You can also connect to Pastor Dudley on *GodHasanApp.com*, *CallonJesus.com*, and *theshepherd.org*

# OTHER PUBLISHED WORKS BY
## DUDLEY RUTHERFORD

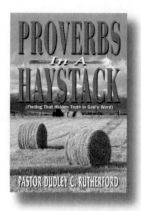

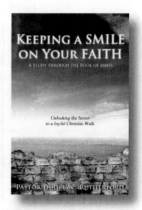

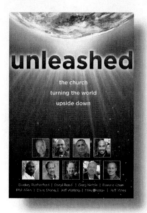

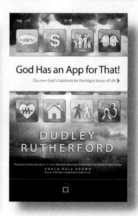

Visit www.callonjesus.com to discover more books by Pastor Dudley Rutherford including *Proverbs in a Haystack* – a reference guide for finding the treasures of Proverbs conveniently organized by subjects we all experience, *Romancing Royalty* which includes 365 devotions designed to draw you closer to Jesus, *Keeping a Smile On Your Faith* – a fascinating study on the book of James, *Unleashed* which includes the perspectives of eight other dynamic men of God and is a call for the church to take a bold stand for truth and holiness, and *God Has an App for That* which reassures us that God knows the issues we face every day and has the time-honored advice, counsel and wisdom to make our lives more meaningful.

## www.CallOnJesus.com